Embracing Ambiguity

Embracing Ambiguity

A Workforce Training Plan for the Postpandemic Economy

Michael Edmondson, PhD

BEP

BUSINESS EXPERT PRESS

Leader in applied, concise business books

Embracing Ambiguity:
A Workforce Training Plan for the Postpandemic Economy

Cover design by Divya Pidaparti

Interior design by Exeter Premedia Services Private Ltd., Chennai, India

First published in 2021 by
Business Expert Press, LLC
222 East 46th Street, New York, NY 10017
www.businessexpertpress.com

ISBN-13: 978-1-63742-171-0 (paperback)
ISBN-13: 978-1-63742-172-7 (e-book)

Business Expert Press Human Resource Management and Organizational Behavior Collection

Collection ISSN: 1946-5637 (print)
Collection ISSN: 1946-5645 (electronic)

First edition: 2021

10 9 8 7 6 5 4 3 2 1

Description

Embracing Ambiguity: A Workforce Training Plan for the Postpandemic Economy fills a tremendous need in today's chaotic marketplace by providing a timely, impactful, and relevant self-directed training program designed to enhance the essential skills employees need to embrace the ambiguity of a postpandemic world. In today's dynamic, hyper-competitive, and ever-changing global economy organizations need to make investing in the personal growth and professional development of its employees a strategic imperative. Doing so requires organizations to think differently about training its workforce, adapt new strategies of employee engagement, and create a more agile approach to human capital management. Since the new reality is that life in a postpandemic world will look different than it did prior to the global health care crisis employees should be encouraged to engage in a self-directed training program to enhance their future potential. Such a program provides employees with the opportunity to learn at their own pace, in a safe environment, and at a convenient time of day. By shifting the locus of control over to the employee, individuals maintain the self-determination required to identify, develop, and enhance the essential skills necessary to embrace the ambiguity in a postpandemic world. By engaging in self-directed learning employees will increase their self-awareness, further their sense of the world around them, and reflect on the intersection of the two. Required reading for individuals from small-to-medium sized businesses, large corporations, nonprofit organizations, and government offices, *Embracing Ambiguity* offers employers and employees alike a valuable resource to use as they chart a course forward in a postpandemic marketplace.

Keywords

change; management; manager; business; leadership; employee training

Contents

Preface

The Relevance of History to the Present

In April 1928, *The Forum* journal published an interview with American industrialist and business magnate Henry Ford who commented on the apparent increase in the complexity and rapidity of life. The 1920s, also known as the "Roaring Twenties," witnessed a decade of economic growth and widespread prosperity resulting in an unprecedented period of social, artistic, and cultural dynamics propelling Americans into the era of modernity. But Ford was skeptical about whether there had been a commensurate increase in thought during the decade's advancements. According to Ford "But there is a question in my mind whether, with all this speeding up of our everyday activities, there is any more real thinking. Thinking is the hardest work there is, which is the probable reason why so few engage in it."[1] In his seminal 1936 publication *The General Theory of Employment, Interest and Money*, English economist John Maynard Keynes echoed similar sentiment when he wrote "The difficulty lies not so much in developing new ideas as in escaping from old ones."[2] To sustain growth, relevance, and vitality in the near future, individuals, organizations, and governments around the world will need to think differently, challenge assumptions, and embrace the ambiguity of the postpandemic world. The local, national, and global challenges will demand that people everywhere "escape old ideas and embrace new ones" and engage in "hard work involved with thinking."

One recent resource illustrating global issues in the postpandemic world is the 16th edition of the *Global Risks Report*, published in January 2021 by the World Economic Forum (WEF). The WEF recommended "more innovative and collaborative approaches to resilience are needed to address the disruptive implications of major global risks, including the coronavirus disease (COVID)-19 pandemic, ongoing geopolitical and societal challenges, and the existential crisis of climate change."[3] The intention of this publication is to contribute in some small way to the innovative approaches needed for individuals and organizations to remain relevant in the volatile, uncertain, complex, and ambiguous (VUCA) postpandemic future. Commenting on the need for organizations to envision a new future, Tim Allen wrote in an April 7, 2021, *Harvard Business Review* article that in the postpandemic environment, "our new normal does not have to look like the old one; in fact, it is better if it did not."[4] This current need for innovative solutions will only increase as the problems of today give way to the issues of tomorrow. According to the WEF, the following critical threats and time-horizons will contribute to the postpandemic VUCA environment during the next decade.

- The next two years (2021–2023): employment and livelihood crises, widespread youth disillusionment, digital inequality, economic stagnation, human-made environmental damage, erosion of societal cohesion, and terrorist attacks.
  - Example: The Organization for Economic Co-operation and Development (OECD) area unemployment rate declined in February 2021, to 6.7% (from 6.8% in January), remaining 1.4 percentage points above the level observed in February 2020, before the COVID-19 pandemic hit the labor market.[5] The OECD is an inter-governmental economic organization with 38 member countries, founded in 1961 to stimulate economic progress and world trade.
- The next three to five years (2024–2026): economic risks including asset bubbles, price instability, commodity shocks and debt crises; followed by geopolitical risks, including inter-state relations and conflict, and resource geo-politization.
  - Example: As James Berman wrote in an April 01, 2021, *Forbes* column "It's time for a reckoning in bubble assets. Not since 1999 have I seen so much garbage trading at such crazy prices."[6] That's when the Nasdaq reached 5048 before declining 80%." Moreover, in September 2020, the United Nations published a report *Shaping the Trends Our Times* and stated that interstate relations, conflict, and resource geo-politization are inevitable as long as humans continue to act and interact with each other around the globe.[7]

- The five-to-ten-year horizon (2026–2031): environmental risks such as biodiversity loss, natural resource crises and climate action failure dominate, alongside weapons of mass destruction, adverse effects of technology, and collapse of states or multilateral institutions.
  - Example: The European Commission plans to unveil far-reaching regulations to limit technologies powered by artificial intelligence (AI).[8] Released on April 21, 2021, the EU's proposed AI regulation poses a direct challenge to Silicon Valley's common view that law should leave emerging technology alone. "The proposal sets out a nuanced regulatory structure that bans some uses of AI, heavily regulates high-risk uses and lightly regulates less risky AI systems."[9]

To prepare for these and other future crises, individuals, organizations, and societies around the world would be best served by challenging their assumptions to think differently and leverage the past to apply lessons to the present. The need to challenge assumptions and think differently will create the necessary "paradigm shift" Frank Swiaczny, a German demographer and former chief of population trends and analysis for the United Nations, called for when asked how world leaders should address the projected decline in global population. For Swiaczny, "countries need to learn to live with and adapt to population decline."[10] The projected downward trend in population growth, like most of the other global dynamics will continue to present unpredicted questions, issues, and challenges. Leveraging one's ability to think differently can provide the necessary spark to find answers and solutions. To aid the paradigm shift and help one think differently, individuals should recall the words of English writer and philosopher Aldous Huxley who observed "That men do not learn very much from the lessons of history is the most important of all the lessons of history."[11] The ability for individuals to couple a paradigm shift with applied lessons of history, however, marks a truly valuable option for anyone looking to embrace ambiguity in the postpandemic world.

This publication reflects my lifelong dedication of illustrating the relevance of history and extracting its value for application to the present. Various interpretations of Huxley's axiom center around the theme of "those who do not learn from history are doomed to repeat it." But to abbreviate his observation is to short change the relevance, vitality, and vibrancy of history. Far beyond the nomenclature of names, dates, and facts, history provides great meaning for those willing to excavate its complexities, nuances, and dynamics. Since the greatest lesson is that individuals fail to learn from history one must ask any number of questions starting with "why?" Why is there a perpetual failure to learn from the past? What is preventing people from learning the lessons of history? When shall the learning begin? My suggestion is now. For those wishing to remain relevant in the postpandemic world, this publication provides a training program built upon learning from the lessons of history. Failing to do so only jeopardizes one's ability to navigate the VUCA landscape. There is no going back to "normal." In the postpandemic VUCA world, "legacy thinking, antiquated leadership styles, and many management practices from the past will no longer cut it."[12] Therefore, a new approach to just about everything is required. Ignoring the skills, traits, and habits of others who found a way forward during turbulent times in the past will only make our recovery from COVID-19 more difficult. Learning from the lessons of those who embraced the ambiguity of their life situation can provide us with moonlight when there is darkness. A PhD in history allows one to become both a specialist in a narrow field of study and then a generalist for thousands of other topics.

Leveraging the space between specialist and generalist afforded me the opportunity to create, identify, and explain an Essential Skill set and related historical references required to embrace the ambiguity of the postpandemic world. The stories, assessments, and questions included in this publication are grounded in what historian Peter N. Stearns labeled "the laboratory of human experience" and are designed to serve as a reference guide for any organization or individual interested in thriving and remaining relevant in the postpandemic society.[13] As society awakens to the postpandemic morning and rises from its slumber of isolation, it can find guidance on how to navigate the path forward from those who have done so in the past. Let us remember the lessons of history. The COVID-19 global pandemic was tragic on many levels. But it was not the only tragic period in world history. Let us leverage the lessons of history to propel us forward. And let us realize this journey to emerge into the postpandemic world is just one of many, we will travel navigating the chaos of life. History is filled with nonfictional accounts, and fictional characters that serve as reference points for those looking to learn how to embrace ambiguity. For example, a recent illustration came in the form of the first season, second episode of the HBO Max series *Hacks*, released in May 2021 when Deborah Vance (portrayed by Jean Smart) as a legendary Las Vegas comedian, is stuck in the desert with her 25-year-old writer Ava (portrayed by Hannah Einbinder). After Ava talks about how good she is and cries about life being so hard, Deborah turns to her and raises her voice telling Ava "Good is the minimum. It's the baseline. You have to be so much more than good. And even if you're great and lucky, you still have work really hard."[14] But as the Deborah Vances throughout history and the world understand first-hand, "And even that is not enough. You have to scratch and claw, and it never ends."[15]

If you want to embrace the ambiguity of the postpandemic world, you will, like so many others before you, have to be so much more than good. You will need to work really hard all the time. As the tragic events of the COVID-19 global pandemic slowly fade from the collective global memory, you will still need to "scratch and claw since it never ends." But this training program is designed to help those willing to put in the requisite time, effort, and reflection. *Embracing Ambiguity* provides you with a self-directed learning training program built upon the foundation that professional development is linked to personal growth. If you want to grow as a professional you will need to grow as a person. Dale Chihuly understood this. Two events transformed Chihuly's life. The prominent 20th century glass sculptor was involved in a 1976 traffic accident that blinded his left eye and three years later he dislocated his right shoulder in a bodysurfing accident. These two events prohibited Chihuly from holding the pipe involved with glass blowing. Not to be deterred he hired others to do the work. Unable to create the glass art, he taught others and learned how to become "more choreographer than dancer, more supervisor than participant, more director than actor."[16] He thought differently, worked really hard, embraced the ambiguity of his situation, and went on to have a wildly successful career.

This book is divided into two parts. The first section provides a situational analysis of the emerging postpandemic environment through a brief assessment of five key topics. Chapter 1 summarizes an assessment of the pandemic's ongoing impact around the world. Chapter 2 highlights how various individuals and organizations leveraged agility to embrace the ambiguity of the pandemic. Chapter 3 focuses on the significance of self-awareness afforded to individuals due to the restrictions imposed on them as a result of the pandemic. People had more time to reflect upon their life and, as a result, significant new trends started to emerge. Chapter 4 illustrates how ambiguity had already been in existence prior to the pandemic due to the dynamics present in today's VUCA global marketplace. The last chapter in part one introduces the essential skills required to compliment the traditional hard and soft skills employees across industries, positions, and functions utilize.

Part two introduces the 10 Essential Skills that form the foundation of the Embracing Ambiguity training program as well as a variety of exercises, questions, and assessments. The Essential Skills compliment the traditional hard and soft skills so often identified as key to one's professional and personal development. The 10 Essential Skills focus on both the physical and cognitive options available to people as they look to embrace the ambiguity of the postpandemic world. To recognize just how prevalent ambiguity is as a global dynamic, individuals can accept the existence and permanence of chaos (Essential Skill 1) that will, in turn, help them challenge their assumptions and think differently (Essential Skill 2). By considering different viewpoints individuals can help themselves connect and empower others (Essential Skill 3). Moreover, embracing the ambiguity will require a good deal of effort, so it will be imperative to demonstrate a strong work ethic (Essential Skill 4) while simultaneously experimenting with life (Essential Skill 5). To experiment, however, one will need to travel outside their comfort zone (Essential Skill 6) that, in turn, will require one to consider managing their stress and anxiety (Essential Skill 7). By recognizing and understanding the role of nuance in decision making (Essential Skill 8), individuals wishing to embrace the ambiguity of the postpandemic world have the power to both remain open to the unfolding of life (Essential Skill 9) and remind themselves destiny is a matter of choice (Essential Skill 10).

All the best,

—Michael Edmondson, PhD

PART I

The Situational Analysis

CHAPTER 1

The Impact of COVID-19

In January 2020, as reports of COVID-19 were emerging from China and elsewhere, the World Bank forecasted global economic expansion at 2.5 percent for the year. By January 2021, a mere 12 months later, "with the pandemic still holding much of the world in its grip, the World Bank estimated that the global economy contracted by 4.3% in 2020, a turnabout of 6.8 percentage points."[1] Any discussion of the impact of COVID-19, and the postpandemic world, requires a brief understanding of viruses and the diseases. To begin with, viruses and diseases are related but have different names. For example, a virus that emerged during the 1980s and is now commonly referred to as human immunodeficiency virus (HIV) causes the disease known as acquired immunodeficiency syndrome (AIDS). Thus, HIV is the virus and AIDS is the disease. People are often familiar with the name of a disease but less likely to know the name of the virus causing it. According to the World Health Organization (WHO), there are different processes and purposes for naming viruses and diseases.[2] To facilitate the development of diagnostic tests, vaccines, and medicines, viruses are named by the International Committee on Taxonomy of Viruses (ICTV). Diseases are named to enable discussion on disease prevention, spread, transmissibility, severity, and treatment and are named by the WHO's International Classification of Diseases (ICD).

On February 11, 2020, ICTV announced "severe acute respiratory syndrome coronavirus 2 (SARS-CoV-2)" as the name of the new virus. On the same day, the WHO's ICD announced "COVID-19" as the name of the disease caused by the newly identified virus.[3] With its mission to "promote worldwide health, keep the world safe, and serve the vulnerable," WHO held over 120 media briefings during 2020, "involving international expert networks, covering topics such as clinical management, laboratory and virology, infection prevention and control, mathematical modeling, seroepidemiology, and research and development for diagnostics, therapeutics, and vaccines."[4] As of May 27, 2021, and according to the COVID-19 Dashboard by the Center for Systems Science and Engineering at Johns Hopkins University, 113,950,840 people around the world were diagnosed with COVID and, sadly over 3.5 million people died during the pandemic, including over 592,000 in the United States.[5] The pandemic's impact was felt in almost every corner of the globe, sending shockwaves throughout the world's political, economic, financial, social, educational, and environmental systems.

The World Economic Forum declared "The immediate human and economic cost of COVID-19 is severe. It threatens to scale back years of progress on reducing poverty and inequality and to further weaken social cohesion and global cooperation."[6] While it remains too early to define the extent of global damage caused by the COVID-19 novel coronavirus pandemic, "there is widespread agreement among economists that it will have severe negative impacts on the global economy."[7] Noting the significant impact COVID had on the global population, the BBC wrote in a January 24, 2021 article, "The coronavirus pandemic has reached almost every country in the world. Its spread has left national economies and businesses counting the costs while many are still wondering what recovery could look like."[8] Commenting on the sudden and severe disruption COVID caused around the world, the global consulting firm McKinsey added "millions of people were furloughed or lost jobs, and others rapidly adjusted to working from home as offices closed. Many other workers were deemed essential and continued to work in hospitals and grocery stores, on garbage trucks and in warehouses, yet under new protocols to reduce the spread of the novel coronavirus."[9]

In February 2021, the International Monetary Fund (IMF) estimated a 4.4 percent drop in the global economy for 2020. If that holds true, such a decrease "would be the worst annual plunge since the Great Depression of the 1930s. By comparison, the international economy contracted by a far smaller 0.1% after the devastating 2008 financial crisis."[10] IMF foresees "limited progress toward catching up to the path of economic activity for 2020–25 projected before the pandemic for both advanced and emerging market and developing economies. The pandemic is also causing a severe setback to the projected improvement in average living standards across all country groups and will reverse the progress made since the 1990s in reducing global poverty by increasing inequality."[11] In March 2021, the Pew Research Center published a report stating "the global middle class encompassed 54 million fewer people in 2020 than projected prior to the pandemic; while the number of poor is estimated to have been 131 million higher because of the concurrent global recession."[12] The United States experienced similar setbacks as other countries around the world did during COVID.

On the challenges business leaders must confront in the postpandemic marketplace, Deloitte identified climate change, geopolitical stability, increasing societal expectations, and of course, world health to name a few.[13] For those willing to embrace agility, however, business leaders can address many of the pandemic-related implications and learn to leverage the postpandemic environment as a springboard to future success. Even though the pandemic's impact on the U.S. economy is far from final, a December 2020 report published by researchers with the University of Southern California concluded "the COVID-19 pandemic could result in net losses from $3.2 trillion and up to $4.8 trillion in U.S. real gross domestic product (GDP) over the course of two years."[14] "The pandemic's economic impact depends on factors such as the duration and extent of the business closures, the gradual reopening process, infection rates and fatalities, avoiding public places, and pent-up consumer demand."[15] In total, 25.1 million workers—or 14.7 percent of the workforce—have been directly harmed by the coronavirus downturn.[16] According to the Economic Policy Institute, it would take more than two years to even get back to prerecession employment levels.[17] Women were particularly hurt by the pandemic. As of February 2021, women were still down 5.4 million jobs from February 2020, before the pandemic began, as compared to 4.4 million job losses for men. Women "started 2020 on roughly equal footing, with women holding 50.03% of jobs, but ended it holding 860,000 fewer jobs than their male peers."[18] Specifically, Black and Latina women suffered a disproportionate amount of job losses during the pandemic since they worked in some of the hardest-hit sectors and often in roles that lack paid sick leave and the ability to work from home. With little flexibility in their employment positions and sectors, Black and Latina women, according to C. Nicole Mason, president, and CEO of the Institute for Women's Policy Research, "were unable to work because of caregiving responsibilities and had to exit the workforce."[19] In addition to workers, small business owners also experienced extreme hardship during the pandemic. According to the Service Corps of Retired Executives report published in December 2020, many U.S. small businesses failed to turn a profit during the year. "In fact, just 34 percent of small business owners said that their operations are currently profitable while 55 percent were profitable back in 2019."[20]

While COVID dramatically altered almost every aspect of life in 2020 continuing into 2021, it did so in a global environment that was already labeled as volatile, uncertain, complex, and ambiguous (VUCA). VUCA refers to the world as it is now and as it develops. Thus it is VUCA now, and will continue to be so. Another way to think about VUCA is that it refers to the modern way to speak about change and the need to adapt to change. As Wanda Tiefenbacher noted, "VUCA is a reality that is not new—rather, the VUCA world as we know it is merely one snippet of an ever-changing, ever-growing, and ever-evolving environment."[21] The U.S. Army War College coined the term VUCA in the late 1980s to describe the volatility, uncertainty, complexity, and ambiguity of the post-Cold War world. Here is a brief definition of each word:

- *Volatility*: refers to the rate of change related to an unexpected event or series of events. The more volatile in the world the greater things change. For example, in January 2021, Tyler Cowen reflected upon what the new year might look like and wrote "2021 will be better than 2020, but the year's defining feature will be volatility."[22]
- *Uncertainty*: refers to the extent to which individuals can confidently predict the future. The greater the volatility, the more difficult it is to suggest specific outcomes. Commenting on the role uncertainty plays in planning, researchers Alain Govaert and Ming Cao noted "many of today's most pressing societal concerns require decisions which take into account a distant and uncertain future."[23]
- *Complexity*: refers to the number, variety, and relationships of factors involved. The ability to understand a situation

is directly proportional to the number of factors involved; that is, the larger the number of factors the greater the difficulty in understanding the situation. Joanna Boehnert, Lecturer in Design and the Creative Industries of Loughborough University, created "The Visual Representations of Complexity" to illustrate 16 key features of complex systems. Doing so helps leaders understand the depths of uncertainty, the multitude of variables involved, and the overwhelming complexity organizations must address in a VUCA world.[24]

- *Ambiguity*: refers to a lack of clarity about how to interpret something. A situation is ambiguous, for example, when information is incomplete, contradicting, or too inaccurate to draw definite conclusions. More generally it refers to fuzziness and vagueness in ideas and terminology. Commenting on the relationship between ambiguity and leadership, Adam Bryant noted "Ambiguous times are no time for ambiguous leadership and with so many employees working remotely, leaders must take extra care to ensure their communications leave no room for misinterpretation."[25]

The literature on VUCA continues to grow with each passing year. Examples of books include Don Gilman, *Outsmarting VUCA: Achieving Success in a Volatile, Uncertain, Complex, & Ambiguous World*, Ann V. Deaton, *VUCA Tools for a VUCA World: Developing Leaders and Teams for Sustainable Results*, and Michael Fuchs, Jochen Messner, and Rob Sok, *Leadership in a VUCA World*.[26] Moreover, the reports, data, and articles focused on VUCA are numerous, readily available, and published on a regular basis. The VUCA resources generally have one theme in common—change. As an illustration of how VUCA has grown as a primary descriptor of today's global marketplace, the bar chart in Figure 1.1 details the approximate number of years it took for 25 percent of the U.S. population to adopt new technology from electricity (45 years) to smartphones (5 years). Internet usage around the world provides another perspective of the global reach involved with the volatility, uncertainty, complexity, and ambiguity of today and tomorrow.

Technology Adoption Rate ~25% of U.S. population

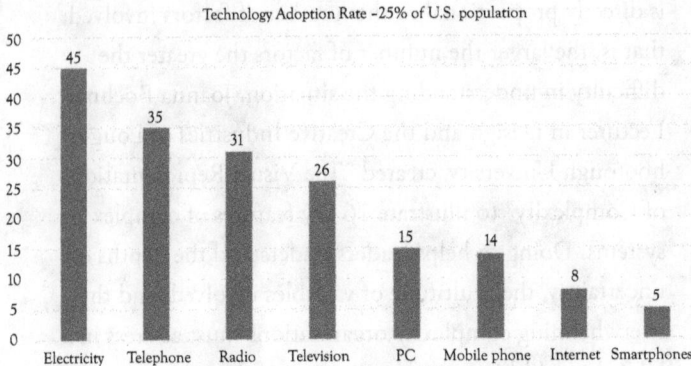

Figure 1.1 Number of years it took for 25 percent of the U.S. population to adopt

Global internet usage has grown significantly during the last two decades. As of December 30, 2020, 64.7 percent of the global population had Internet access. In raw numbers, this means that 5.1 billion people, out of the global population of 7.8 billion, are online.[27] In the United States, 89.8 percent of the population has Internet access. In raw numbers that equals 297 million out of the 369 million people across the United States.[28] According to Visual Capitalist, "In 2020 the world changed fundamentally and so did the data that makes the world go round."[29] In the eighth edition of its Data Never Sleeps Report published in September 2020, Visual Capitalist noted the significant impact COVID-19 made on nearly every aspect of life. In doing so, people around the world depended more on apps and the Internet than in past years. The Data Never Sleeps Report provides a well-known infographic labeled "What Happens In An Internet Minute." According to the 2020 edition, every minute of every hour of every day in 2020…

- Netflix users streamed 404,444 hours of video.
- Instagram users posted 347,222 stories.
- YouTube users uploaded 500 hours of video.
- Consumers spent $1,000,000 online.
- Facebook users shared 150,000 messages.
- LinkedIn users applied for 69,444 jobs.
- WhatsApp users shared 41,666,667 messages.[30]

The collision of an ongoing VUCA environment with a pandemic spreading around the world created an unprecedented global crisis that opened the collective eyes of leaders, managers, and employees alike to a different way of working. Those companies and organizations looking to sustain long-term growth in the postpandemic period need to align their mission with the adoption of new digital technologies, implement a SMAC (Social, Mobile, Analytics, and Cloud) strategy, and empower employees to embrace the ambiguity of constantly changing realities.[31] Recognizing the new realities postpandemic, Deloitte published "Beyond Reskilling: Unleashing Workforce Potential," and concluded "The most important way organizations can unleash workers' potential is to empower them with agency and choice over what they do … to choose how they can best help tackle critical business problems as organizations evolve."[32] Doing so, requires leadership to develop an agile mindset so their organizations can leverage agility and embrace the ambiguity of the postpandemic global marketplace.

CHAPTER 2

Leveraging Agility

To navigate their way through the intersection of coronavirus disease (COVID) and VUCA, many organizations struggled to manage challenging and unprecedented demands that included redeploying human capital, establishing remote workforces, building needed capabilities, supporting distressed supply chains, deciding whether to retain, furlough, or fire employees, planning for reopening amid uncertainty, and maintaining productivity. Upon reflection, researchers have started to draw several conclusions about this collision of COVID in a VUCA world and the subsequent responses at the societal and organizational levels such as "a lack of preparedness, a deficit in capabilities, and silence on structural inequality were three implications."[1] For example, in their research published in December 2020, Eric Garton and Michael Mankins discovered the productivity gap between the best companies and the rest widened during the pandemic. The best companies experienced a productivity growth of 5 to 8 percent while most organizations experienced a net reduction in productivity of 3 to 6 percent (or more) due to inefficient collaboration, wasteful ways of working, and an overall decline in employee engagement."[2] Successfully increasing productivity during the stress of a global pandemic will allow an organization to better prepare for the future and "enable organizations to out-team, out-innovate, outgrow, and outperform their competitors for many years."[3]

Commenting on the complexities involved with leading in a VUCA world, General George W. Casey, Jr., U.S. Army (Retired) observed "We live in a connected but unstable world where stability is the passing phase, instability is the norm, and complexity is accumulating. Things change quickly, and for reasons beyond our control."[4] This lack of control creates an environment of uncertainty increasing in complexity with each passing day. Therefore, leaders in the postpandemic and VUCA global marketplace must accept the realization they will most likely never know the interaction of the multiple variables to consider, the proper methods to integrate them effectively, or how to consider the spectrum of competing interpretations of available data. It is imperative then, that leaders and managers alike make defining reality for their people a top priority. Rest assured, employees will be searching for a definition of reality and if their management team lacks a cohesive explanation, the employees will either make up their own definition or go elsewhere for one. In short, "denying reality makes people assume their leader is either lying or out of touch."[5]

Take for example the tremendous disconnect in higher education where "96% of chief academic officers say their institution is 'very or somewhat' effective at preparing students for the world of work but only 11% of business leaders strongly agree."[6] As Brandon Busted from Gallup concluded "There is clearly a massive disconnect between higher education and the marketplace in terms of what it means to be prepared for work."[7] If higher education institutions, or any organization for that matter, want to remain relevant and successfully navigate challenges in the postpandemic environment, their leaders must focus on solutions and "be honest with their people to a level that will and should feel uncomfortable."[8] The evidence suggests that higher education leaders have a tremendous amount of work to do if they are to communicate and clear, concise, and compelling definition of reality to their campuses. Anything short of this will make it difficult for colleges and universities to embrace the ambiguity associated with today's postpandemic and VUCA world.

"Since the 21st century will see a rising tide of new technologies, some of which are now emerging and some of which will surprise us,"[9] leveraging agility to embrace ambiguity will be critical for those organizations seeking a sustainable future. Disruption is far from over as Brian Kropp wrote in a January 14, 2021, *Harvard Business Review* post "While 2020 was the most volatile year in modern history, we need to understand as we move into 2021 and beyond, the rate of disruption will potentially accelerate as the implications from 2020 play out across the next several years."[10] This is particularly true when it comes to the employment picture across the nation. On February 2, 2021, the Congressional Budget Office (CBO) reported the number of employed Americans is not expected to return to its prepandemic level until 2024. The CBO did report, however, that it expects the broader U.S. economy to have a full recovery by the middle of 2021.[11] If one thing is clear, "there is no going back to the pre-pandemic workplace. Organizations and individuals have had no choice but to discover new ways of working."[12] Perhaps the most significant implication to emerge in the postpandemic world is the paradigm shift involving where people work and the related challenge employers have "to create a work environment that optimizes flexibility for employees, but also facilitates maximum productivity."[13] For example, employers have started to look beyond job titles in order to map out essential functions and activities and reimagine work flows as they anticipate tomorrow's workplaces and the expectations of tomorrow's workforces.[14]

The pandemic-related paradigm shift continues to send ripples throughout organizations from small- and medium-sized businesses to large corporations and nonprofits. Ashira Gobrin noted this change in a February 23, 2021, *Forbes* article stating "We're going through a paradigm shift in the workplace. What was once a primarily in-office model has transformed into a remote-first working environment."[15] For example, a global study by Slack published in October 2020 found that 72 percent of knowledge workers said they would prefer a mix of remote and office work, with the rest split evenly between a preference for working exclusively from the office or exclusively from home.[16] Additionally, since organizations have had positive experiences with employees working remotely during the pandemic, some are already planning to shift to flexible workspaces post pandemic. Such a move will reduce the overall space organizations need and bring fewer workers into offices each day. A survey of 278 executives by McKinsey in August 2020 found that on average, organizations planned to reduce office space by 30 percent.[17]

Reflecting on the road ahead Avrom Goldberg noted in January 2021 "The first global pandemic in over a century has upended many of the few certainties left to us in our personal and professional lives. And just one month into 2021, as the promise of vaccines and the threat of new strains fill the headlines, the future has never seemed more nebulous."[18] Collectively, people are not accustomed to the level of uncertainty thrust upon them by the COVID pandemic.[19] The transition to the postpandemic world will be far from seamless as individuals have complex questions to consider as they determine a path forward.[20] Therefore, the postpandemic world requires leaders, employees, and stakeholders alike to leverage agility and embrace the ambiguity of an uncertain future. To thrive in today's ambiguous environment, Mark Esposito has argued leaders need to become agile, fluid, and dynamic to approach uncertainty as an opportunity for growth.[21] The Irish economic and social philosopher Charles Handy said, "Whereas the heroic manager of the past knew all, could do all, and could solve every problem, the post-heroic manager asks how every problem can be solved in a way that develops other people's capacity to handle it."[22]

To achieve and sustain growth in an uncontrollable environment permeated by disruption, turbulence, and flux, author Susan Cranston suggested leaders now need to demand a higher importance be placed on trust-building and agile problem-solving skills."[23] Tom O'Shea, Principal and Organizational Agility Practice Leader in Agility Consulting & Training echoed a similar thought and observed "2020 was a definite example of VUCA on steroids; 2021 hopefully will be less turbulent and disruptive, but we can expect it to continue to accelerate and separate the agile from the fragile."[24] Individuals can leverage the Essential Skills included in this training program to help themselves embrace ambiguity and work toward being agile, an oft touted trait. For example, in its "2021 CEO Study: Find Your Essential," IBM noted the unprecedented need for leaders to become agile in order to respond quickly and pivot without losing momentum and found that 56 percent of CEOs emphasized the need to "aggressively pursue" operational agility and flexibility over the next two to three years.[25]

As Piyush Gupta, CEO, DBS Bank observed "If you can embrace agile setups and experiments, and constantly nurture a learning culture, then you become adaptive and nimble."[26] On this need to experiment in order to become adaptive and nimble, researchers from Massachusetts Institute of Technology (MIT) noted the postpandemic workplace "provides an unprecedented opportunity to explore and experiment. Leaders must learn to continually reinvent the future of work, and now is the time to begin discovering how to bring about that future."[27] For those leaders skeptical of developing agility, they should refer to the April 2021 report published by Deloitte entitled "Agility: The Antidote to Complexity" that concluded "agility is an antidote that helps inoculate firms against complexity and risk so that they deliver healthy performance results even in the toughest of times; and building agility is not a distraction to delivering performance; it's a critical enabler."[28] To guide leaders, Deloitte created an "agility index" of capabilities practiced by "agility masters" such as level of alignment to changing stakeholder objectives and metrics, supply market intelligence to improve sensing and prediction, and predictive analytics and advanced technology to improve rapid decision making to name a few.[29]

There is a plenty of evidence to suggest some companies developed significant agility on the fly during the pandemic. Necessity, as the adage goes, is truly the cause of invention. The innovations created during the pandemic were not part of a strategic plan, were not built into compensation systems, were not led by senior leaders, and nor did they go through the usual stage-gate process.[30] As researchers published in the *Harvard Business Review*, agile thinking that produced an innovative solution during the pandemic was often the result of "a small group of people who spotted an urgent need, dropped lower-priority activities, broke typical bureaucratic procedures, and transformed from everyday workers to real-life corporate MacGyvers, surprising themselves and their bosses in the process."[31] To develop their inner MacGyvers, Martin Emrich wrote for the American Management Association and noted "being a leader in the VUCA world means leaders need to realize rigid long-term planning does not always make sense, rely on their courage more for testing new ideas, and emphasize learning while doing."[32] Doing so can help a leader embrace the ambiguity of a postpandemic world, and in so doing, demonstrate the same to others in the organization. While some organizations shifted to a more agile approach, many others failed to do so and, therefore, struggled to find innovative solutions.

This struggle existed, according to Helio Borges, because there is still a dire need for managers to stop solving problems using antiquated thinking, begin understanding how to lead in complex systems times, and build the necessary new competencies for leaders and employees alike to embrace the ambiguity of a postpandemic world.[33] Sunil Prashara,

President and CEO of PMI proclaimed "In a world of constant change, organizations need to go even farther than agility and become what we called 'gymnastic'—capable of pivoting and making rapid changes and embracing a wide variety of project approaches to meet the challenge."[34] One such area that will require a "gymnastic" approach is employee engagement. "Designing an employee experience for everyone post-pandemic is a strategic imperative for leaders who want to maintain their workforce and inspire them to be the best version of themselves so that both they and the business can thrive."[35] Such creativity requires leaders to leverage a mental model built on a set of assumptions that anything can happen coupled with a belief in their inability to predict the future. To that end and writing in *Forbes* on May 4, 2021 Shama Hyder noted "despite vaccines and plans to return to the office, businesses can only thrive with preparation, an agile team, and those who can remain fearless in the age of pivots."[36] Moreover, Beth Tyner Jones asked the question "there is a place past COVID-19—how will we prepare for it? and suggested the answers will determine which companies emerge from the pandemic ready to thrive and which ones will continue to struggle."[37] Such emergence requires leaders accept the omnipresence of disruption and assess their organization's operations and policies to measure how they meet the needs of the postpandemic workforce, create a workplace designed for the times, and invite employees to engage in the training required to embrace ambiguity.

In the postpandemic marketplace employers and employees both need to realize that "disruption has become the norm more than anything else" and that sustainability requires agile, customer-centric, and change-orientated cultures.[38] For example, in its April 2021 publication "A US Workforce Training Plan for the Post pandemic Economy." The Conference Board reported "Static job definitions and management within organizations can no longer keep pace with how fast jobs are evolving. The pace of change demands a workforce of life-long learners who can continually learn and develop new and needed skills."[39] This fast-paced, dynamic, and ever changing postpandemic period is a critical time in modern history for both organizations and employees to proceed with a growth mindset that involves learning, challenging assumptions, and reskilling to make sure individuals are able to sustain their relevance, keep up with the rapid pace of disruption, and prepare for the ambiguous future. Moreover, in the postpandemic world, those wishing to embrace the ambiguity to remain relevant will need to develop "broader skillsets and tools to become changemakers to address the toughest challenges their organizations are facing with."[40] The foundation of which is self-awareness.

CHAPTER 3

The Significance of Self-Awareness

Modern humans, known as *homo sapiens*, appeared ~200,000 years ago when the earliest known anatomically modern human skeletons were found in places such as Omo and Herto in Ethiopia. They represented people with slender body types, high foreheads, and reduced brow ridges compared to Neanderthals or earlier human ancestors.[1] Many human societies transitioned from sustaining on hunting and gathering to sedentary agriculture ~10,000 years ago, domesticating plants and animals, thus enabling the growth of civilization. The emergence of civilizations created the establishment of various forms of government and culture around the world. This development ultimately permitted people to unify within regions and eventually form states and empires. For those last 2,500 years or so, empires had philosophers, sages, and teachers who provided wisdom, knowledge, and observations to guide others on a life well-lived. The art of living well, has been and remains, well, an art. While there are countless books, articles, and other resources examining the huge questions of philosophy from the ancient Greek and Roman philosophers and statesmen, here are six "pearls of wisdom that stand up today as guidelines for living wisely and compassionately."[2] Each statement is followed by one question to upon which to reflect.

- **Heraclitus**—considered the most important pre-Socratic Greek philosopher noted: *No man ever steps in the same river twice, for it's not the same river and he's not the same man.*
    - How often have you thought about how you change over time?

- **Pericles**—a prominent and influential Greek statesman and orator during the Golden Age of Athens observed: *What you leave behind is not what is engraved in stone monuments, but what is woven into the lives of others.*
  - o How often do you think about the implications of your actions and the imprint they might have on those closest to you?
- **Socrates**—**like Plato,** often considered one of the founders of Western logic and philosophy proclaimed: *The only true wisdom is in knowing you know nothing.*
  - o How comfortable are you declaring that you do not know something to yourself or to others?
- **Plato**—like Socrates, often considered one of the founders of Western philosophy said: *The greatest wealth is to live content with little.*
  - o How often do you reflect upon the amount of material you have collected and if you really need it all?
- **Aristotle**—a Greek philosopher also considered one of the founders of Western philosophy wrote: *I count him braver who overcomes his desires than him who conquers his enemies, for the hardest victory is over the self.*
  - o How often do you consider victories over your previous self, more important than declaring a win against someone else?
- **Epictetus**—a Greek sage who was born a slave but gained his freedom, moved to Rome, and began to teach philosophy declared: *Make the best use of what's in your power and take the rest as it happens.*
  - o How often do you make the best use of what is in your power and then take the rest as it happens?

How often should individuals ask themselves these huge questions of philosophy? According to Roman Stoic philosopher Seneca, as often as possible: "It is when times are good that you should prepare yourself for tougher times ahead, for when fortune is kind the soul can build defenses against her ravages."[3] To emphasize the importance of practice

Seneca referred to "soldiers who practice maneuvers in peacetime, erecting bunkers with no enemies in sight and exhausting themselves under no attack so that when it comes, they won't grow tired."[4] Noting the significance of practicing the art of living well, sociobiologist Edward Osborne Wilson, often nicknamed "The Darwin of the 21st Century," argued that "The real problem of humanity is we have paleolithic emotions; medieval institutions; and god-like technology. And it is terrifically dangerous, and it is now approaching a point of crisis overall."[5] Have you ever thought about the intersection of our "paleolithic emotions, medieval institutions, and god-like technology?" But people should think about this. Individuals need to be honest and smart, Wilson stated, so that "we can answer those huge questions of philosophy put forth thousands of years ago: where do we come from? Who are we? Where are we going?"[6] From Seneca's call to Wilson's observation thousands of years later, there has been a constant in the universe for individuals to practice self-reflection and ponder the huge questions of philosophy. Doing so can prepare them for the inevitable periods of stress. Enter the COVID-19 global pandemic and living in quarantine for months. Doing so offered some, certainly not all, an opportunity to reflect on their lives and take advantage of the time to increase their self-awareness by asking those huge questions of philosophy as well as other practical thoughts on life situation and career pathways.

To embrace the ambiguity of a postpandemic VUCA, world individuals should frequently develop, enhance, and reassess their self-awareness. "With self-awareness, a person can make a conscious choice about behavior—they can scan the situation and identify the best behavioral choice."[7] During the pandemic, as people were locked down for weeks or even months at a time, they had the opportunity to ask such questions as "is it time to move to a new location or find a new job?"; "do I want to have my job define who I am?"; and "Do I want to continue to measure my self-worth by my level of productivity?"[8] Self-reflection during the pandemic allowed people to engage in the self-care required to admit that "the things that made them look 'successful' actually made them feel miserable, precarious, or physically unwell."[9] The daily grind in the prepandemic limited the amount of time people devoted to such questions. Perhaps another way of viewing that situation is during the prepandemic world, people did not set aside significant time to ponder life's huge questions. During the pandemic, however, "we've all had a year to evaluate if the life we're living is the one we want to be living," said Christina Wallace, a senior lecturer at Harvard Business School.[10] As Sarah Smalls from Vermont said "It took a pandemic to come along and show me that you don't have a whole lot of time to do what you want to do. It gave me that nudge, and it was a hard nudge."[11]

Noting this behavioral change, Jennifer Levitz wrote in *The Wall Street Journal* "the long pause that forced both isolation and introspection has been a catalyst to change course as people are emerging post-pandemic with new goals, priorities, and concerns."[12] As the pandemic crossed the year-long threshold there evolved a growing amount of evidence that people were reassessing how they lived and worked.[13] A Pew Research Center survey published in February 2021 found 66 percent of unemployed people had "seriously considered" changing their field of work, a far greater percentage than during the 2007 to 2009 Great Recession.[14] People who used to work in restaurants or travel are finding higher-paying jobs in warehouses or real estate, for example. Technically, when workers take a while to figure out what new skills they need, or what jobs they might pivot to, is defined by economists as reallocation friction.[15]

Kevin Roose wrote about this reallocation friction in *The New York Times* on April 21, 2021 and noted "dozens of stories poured into my inboxes, all variations on the same basic theme: *"The pandemic changed my priorities, and I realized I didn't have to live like this."*[16] Further evidence of this new trend came from Prudential's *Pulse of the American Worker Survey* published in April 2021 that found one in five workers changed their line of work entirely over the course of the pandemic.[17] Layoffs, finding better work-life balance, and wanting to try something new where the top three reasons why people changed jobs or careers. Such internal conversations are critical to embracing the ambiguity in a postpandemic world. In an opinion piece published in May 13, 2020 in the *New York Times,* StoryCorps founder Dave Isay commented on the amount of reflection time people had because of the pandemic and wrote "we have more time to reflect on the relationships that really matter in our lives," and proclaimed: "a conversation about life's big questions is the very definition of time well spent."[18]

Numerous examples abound. For example, Miranda Livingston, a 34-year-old project manager in the United Kingdom stated "The pandemic and the lockdowns that swiftly followed have provided us all with a chance to jump off the life treadmill and take a breath, to ponder what our priorities are. Lockdown life is a simpler existence."[19] The pandemic provided author Michele Weldon the opportunity to think about her life: "now in my early 60s-with more life behind me than ahead-I have begun a closer scrutiny of myself, which was a luxury that felt simply inaccessible for many years." COVID-19 infused an urgency into that self-examination.[20] Additionally, Australian Libby Sander, Assistant Professor of Organizational Behavior, Bond University reflected upon the pandemic's impact and realized "not having to go to the office has given me the chance to have some stillness—to be able to have time to think. The fact that we think that's boring is what Covid is really about: the chance to really reset."[21]

So, why then, did it take a global pandemic to remind people to reset and reflect upon life's huge questions? Self-care has been around for a long-time, but the difference is that prepandemic, "it could fall by the wayside if a to-do list got crowded."[22] During the pandemic, the American Psychological Association emphasized the growing importance of self-care even though some people, according to researcher Laura Boxley, "might feel as though self-care is frivolous or selfish in stressful times."[23] F. Diane Barth echoed similar sentiment in *Psychology Today* when she wrote "A major problem for many people is time. With so many other things to do, self-care can feel selfish or indulgent."[24] Nicole Schwarz proposed another theory and wrote many people "have learned to live in chaos and have become comfortable with feeling exhausted and being overworked leaving no time for self-care."[25] According to Kristin Neff, author of *Self-Compassion: The Proven Power of Being Kind to Yourself*, the lack of self-reflection and self-care stemmed from "the great angst of modern life." This angst, according to Neff, consists of a belief held by many: "No matter how hard we try, no matter how successful we are—it's never enough. There is always someone richer, thinner, smarter, or more powerful than we are, someone who makes us feel like a failure in comparison."[26] *Generation Wealth* author and documentary film director Laura Greenfield suggested that this comparison has resulted in a shift in values from "hard work, and thrift, and frugality and modesty" to "bling and showing off and narcissism."[27]

This rise in narcissism has been the subject of Jean Twenge's research. In *Generation Me*, she describes how those born in the 1980s and 1990s are "tolerant, confident, open-minded, and ambitious but also disengaged, narcissistic, distrustful, and anxious." For example, when Twenge examined the narcissism levels of over 15,000 U.S. college students between 1987 and 2006 she discovered 65 percent of modern-day students scored higher in narcissism than previous generations.[28] This change in thought and behavior is illustrated in many reasons, one of which is why young adults report their reasoning to attend college. The portion of incoming freshmen who cited "to be able to get a better job" as a very important reason for attending college reached an all-time high of 87.9 percent in 2012, an increase from 85.9 percent in 2011 and considerably higher than the low of 67.8 percent in 1976. In the minds of today's college students, getting a better job continues to be the most prevalent reason to go to college.[29] But to what end and at what cost? The 2019 scandal over a criminal conspiracy to influence undergraduate admissions decisions at several top American universities would become the apex of just how far wealthy families would go to get their children admitted into a top tier university. As of March 1, 2021, at least 53 people have been charged as part of the conspiracy and 33 parents stand accused of paying more than $25 million between 2011 and 2018 to William Rick Singer, organizer of the scheme, who used part of the money to fraudulently inflate entrance exam test scores and bribe college officials.[30] This scandal, perhaps more than any other, exemplified the growing income inequality in the United States.

Income inequality—the difference between individuals' or households' incomes—has increased in the United States since the 1970s. Rising income inequality is driven largely by relatively rapid income growth at the top of the income distribution. The Congressional Research Service noted in 1975, "the average income of households in the top fifth of income distribution was 10.3 times as large as average household income in the bottom fifth of the distribution; in 2019, average top incomes were 16.6 times as large as those at the bottom."[31] The pandemic only further exacerbated an already substantial income inequality. For example, more than 60 percent of workers with at least a bachelor's degree worked completely from home, versus 20 percent of those with a high school degree or less. Additionally, 39 percent of workers living in a household earning $40,000 or less lost work, compared with 13 percent in those making more than $100,000.[32] To help lessen this gap many researchers emphasize the importance of skill development. For example, a position paper published by the Organization for Economic Co-operation and Development concluded "greater proficiency in key skills among workers drive productivity and participation in the labor force, thus leading to increased growth and prosperity. Reducing the number of low-skilled workers and increasing the number of high-skilled adults is related to social equality."[33] To that end, government at the federal, state, and local levels, according to Edward P. Lazear former chair of the President's Council of Economic Advisers, "should focus on providing the skills necessary to make all workers productive and high-earning members of the modern economy."[34] It is within this context that the modern hard versus soft skill development paradigm exists.

CHAPTER 4

Embracing Ambiguity

The ambiguity of the postpandemic world is merely a continuation of the high degree of uncertainty that existed in the VUCA global environment pre-COVID. As Colonel Eric G. Kail noted in an August 2013 blog post, previous studies on ambiguity have yielded an understanding that "it is one of the leading causes of conflict within a business unit, impossible to diagnose from a singular perspective, and its second- and third-order effects are capable of dismantling an organization."[1] Identifying, assessing, and addressing ambiguity then, is paramount to an organization's sustainability. To diagnose ambiguity within an organization, Kail identified "Two symptoms frequently associated with ambiguity: the inability to accurately conceptualize threats and opportunities before they become lethal and increasing frustration that compartmentalized accomplishments don't add up to comprehensive or enduring success."[2] These symptoms of ambiguity are just two of the many characteristics of modern life that complexity scientist Samuel Arbesman labeled as overcomplicated. In his 2016 book *Overcomplication: Technology at the Limits of Comprehension*, Arbesman argued that survival for both individuals and organizations requires an abandonment of any need for governing principles and rules and accept the chaos.[3]

To address the symptoms of ambiguity and accept the chaos, organizations have relied on the identification, development, and enhancement of hard skills and soft skills. This will continue in the postpandemic marketplace, however, as discussed later, an additional skill set known as Essential Skills, will take precedence. Hard skills include cloud computing, audio production, and data analysis while soft skills focus more on behavior such as communication, creativity, and teamwork. Individuals learn hard skills through education, training, on-the-job experience, and other hands-on learning scenarios. These skills are typically specific to a particular job; for example, accountants need hard skills in mathematics and financial modeling. Other top hard skills required to succeed in a postpandemic world include blockchain, cloud computing, UX design, scientific computing, coding, video production, and data analysis to name a few. In five years, new hard skills will emerge making some of today's current practices obsolete. The one hard skill likely to remain relevant for the foreseeable future is proficiency in Microsoft Office (MS Office). Proficiency in MS Office includes Word, Excel, PowerPoint, and Outlook and demonstrates the ability to make powerful presentations, organize information, and analyze data. As *The Global Training Magazine* noted "MS Office will continue to be a highly sought-after office productivity skill set for many years."[4]

Soft skills, on the other hand, are much harder to quantify than hard skills and refer to an individual's ability to work both on their own and with others.[5] Examples of soft skills needed to succeed in the postpandemic marketplace include empathy, emotional intelligence, integrity, adaptability, resilience, self-motivated, communication, and problem-solving. Developing these and other soft skills are critical for anyone looking to achieve and sustain growth in a postpandemic and VUCA-driven marketplace. Organizations that hire candidates based on the soft skills of adaptability and resilience will have a competitive advantage over those that fail to do so. The VUCA world of tomorrow is only going to increase in disruption, so leaders and employees alike need to remain open-minded so they can shift gears and take on different responsibilities as needed. Doing so will allow them to embrace the ambiguity, adapt their behaviors to their teammates' needs, and manage uncertainty. As Yolanda Lau wrote in *Forbes* "agility and flexibility—which go hand in hand with adaptability—allow workers to bring and implement fresh ideas."[6]

Commenting on the difference in assessment between the two types of skills Bruce Anderson wrote in a January 2020 LinkedIn article "soft skills are typically more difficult to measure, but they can also help a person thrive in a variety of roles and industries."[7] In their 2019 book *Forever skills: The 12 Skills to Future Proof Yourself, Your Team and Your Kids*, authors Kieran Flanagan and Dan Gregory identified 12 soft skills and capabilities everyone needs for the future: Creativity Skills (Insight, Conversion, Problem solving, and Agility); Communication Skills

(Influence, Team building, Trust, and Translation); and Control Skills (Self-control, Resource management, Order and Implementation).[8] Tesla CEO Elon Musk told the audience at the 2019 World Artificial Intelligence Conference in Shanghai "working on skills, especially soft skills, will help you keep your job in the face of increasingly sophisticated automation. Artificial Intelligence will make jobs kind of pointless."[9] Learning new people skills, Musk argued, could help someone remain relevant as more jobs become automated in the future.

Developing new skills should remain a constant for almost every employee regardless of industry, location, or position since "the total number of skills required for a single job is increasing by 10% year over year, and one-third of the skills present in an average 2017 job posting would be outdated by 2021.[10] Moreover, the World Economic Forum estimated that by "2025, over 85 million jobs may be displaced by a shift in the division of labor between humans and machines, while 97 million new roles may emerge that are more adapted to the new division of labor between humans, machines and algorithms."[11] In its February 2021 report "After the Storm: The Jobs and Skills that will Drive the Post-Pandemic Recovery," Burning Glass Technologies identified five Economies, or groups of occupations, positioned for future growth. Burning Glass also projected that employment positions in each of these five Economies would almost double the rate of the job market overall in the United States (15% vs. 8%). Moreover, these five postpandemic growth engines will come to comprise one in six jobs by 2026 (16%). The five Economies are, in no particular order:

- The Readiness Economy (e.g., jobs in biotechnology, cybersecurity, infrastructure, and public health);
- The Logistics Economy (e.g., jobs in industrial big data analytics, Internet of things technologies, and supply chain management);
- The Green Economy (e.g., jobs in renewable energy);
- The Remote Economy (e.g., jobs supporting e-commerce, cloud computing, and network systems); and
- The Automated Economy (e.g., jobs in AI and robotics, software and application development, and data science).[12]

To remain vital, vibrant, and relevant as new jobs replace antiquated positions, leaders and employees alike need to embrace the ambiguity of the postpandemic world and commit to lifelong learning. Fortunately, a few people and organizations are in the vanguard of providing support with skill development. One such person is Beth Cobert who is leading the Rework America Alliance, a national collaboration of organizations working to provide high-quality employment opportunities for millions of unemployed and low-wage workers; particularly people of color, who have been disproportionately affected by the current economic crisis.[13] To help these workers, Cobert believes "employers should really think about the skills that are relevant for a job. They should look for skills, not credentials. They should think differently about writing job descriptions that are focused on skills."[14] This current preference for skills over credentials is actually an extension of previously established prepandemic trends and will likely gain momentum since the number of people attending college plummeted during 2020 and is unlikely to increase anytime soon.[15] For example, in 2015, Karen Cacciattolo published a paper and concluded "formal learning, which consists of degrees, qualifications and certified training, is no longer seen as the sole method of learning while informal learning has become an increasingly important tool for training employees."[16] This structural shift from degrees to skills will add to the ambiguity in a postpandemic world.[17] When asked what leaders could do to help on a personal level, Cobert said they should openly discuss and demonstrate an ability to embrace ambiguity. "Leaders need to role-model how they are wrestling with real choices and they, too, are building their own capabilities."[18] Mark Whittle echoed similar sentiment and said: "As organizations move from their initial pandemic response to more sustainable operations, they are trying to build resilience into everything, from strategy to work design, to enable the organization, its leadership and employees to sense and respond to change, repeatedly."[19] This shift toward a more agile organizational structure existed prior to the pandemic. Today's VUCA world challenged organizations to create flat, nimble, and fluid structures. As Sherrie Haynie noted "the pandemic— the ultimate disruptor—exploded it."[20]

To help organizations build greater resilience into their work force to embrace the ambiguity of a postpandemic VUCA global marketplace, the

Organization for Economic Co-operation and Development (OECD) created a skills compass entitled *The OECD Learning Compass 2030*. To help individuals think differently about skills, this *Learning Compass* expands the hard versus soft paradigm and differentiates skills into three categories: cognitive and meta-cognitive skills, social and emotional skills, as well as physical and practical skills.[21] Metacognition is generally defined as "thinking about thinking, increasing one's self-awareness," developing higher-order thinking skills. Social and emotional skills, such as empathy, self-awareness, respect for others and the ability to communicate, are more relevant as organizations become more ethnically, culturally, and linguistically diverse. Physical and practical skills span the range of taking care of one's physical needs such as cleaning and eating, to the emotional engagement, commitment, and persistence need to overcome life's daily challenges.[22]

As leaders and organizations learn how to embrace the ambiguity of a postpandemic world, "employees are going to need to take ownership of their roles, be entrepreneurial, and will increasingly need to be self-directed 'and captain their own careers relying upon a 'Do-It-Yourself" hacking mentality."[23] Roles and organizations will quickly evolve in the postpandemic world, and as a result, the traditional training methods to develop necessary skills will most likely not exist in the same way. "Employees are going to have to be active participants in identifying the skills, resources, and support they need to do their jobs and collaborate with their companies to get them."[24] The concept of self-directed learning (SDL) is synonymous with having employees be "active participants" in identifying what they need to know to embrace ambiguity and thrive in a postpandemic world. SDL has been around for decades and is often associated with the research of Malcolm Knowles who wrote what is generally considered its standard definition: "SDL describes a process where individuals take the initiative, with or without the help of others, in diagnosing their learning needs, formulating learning goals, identifying resources for learning, choosing and implementing appropriate learning strategies, and evaluating learning outcomes."[25] Due to its reliance on an individual's initiative to diagnose and implement their own learning, SDL is often one of main strategies involved with andragogy, or adult learning.

There are several benefits of implementing SDL, and many of these advantages translate to improved bottom line for an organization.[26] First, SDL gives adult learners the flexibility to schedule and learn whenever and however it is convenient for them to do so. Second, SDL aligns perfectly with the natural learning style of adult learners who do not want to be spoon-fed by teachers. Finally, as SDL facilitates learning according to one's needs, it increases in relevance, and motivates employees to learn from their own experiences while applying their newly acquired knowledge to their job. With the acceleration of change, competition, and disruption expected to continue, SDL will remain a critical strategy for individuals to be life-long learners and develop the critical soft and hard skills required to sustain long-term growth in an uncertain future. As Catherine Lombardozzi noted, "In a world of constant change, learning is as necessary as breathing and each person needs to take personal responsibility for the learning important to them."[27] This necessity for SDL is especially true since "roughly seven in ten people around the world are currently in jobs where their future is ambiguous at best."[28] This ambiguity of future jobs exists, according to *New York Times* columnist and best-selling author Thomas Friedman, "because the pace of technological change, digitization and globalization just keeps accelerating."[29] Soft and hard skills are becoming "obsolete faster and faster resulting in the half-life of skills steadily shrinking."[30] Even before COVID-19 some researchers estimated 40 percent of soft and hard skills required for a given role today would be obsolete within a few years. The pandemic is accelerating that trend.[31]

While some soft and hard skills lose their utility others, such as communication, resilience, and innovation will remain in high-demand.[32] To facilitate the continued growth of soft and hard skills among their employees, leaders need to maintain a growth mindset as it will help them build what Deloitte labeled as "critical new competencies—leading through change, embracing ambiguity, and uncertainty."[33] Recognizing the need businesses have to search for increasingly agile skill sets to stay competitive, JD Dillon wrote "leaders must find ways to provide flexible learning opportunities for a myriad of roles without substantial costs or administration so their organization can keep pace and demonstrate value."[34] For employees and organizations alike to thrive in a postpandemic world marked by rapid change, continued technological disruption, and increased hyper-connectedness lifelong learning will be paramount.[35] On the necessity of lifelong learning, *The Upskilling Imperative* author Shelley Osborne noted "Lifelong learning is not new, and while people are usually open to learning, the constant challenge is to help people understand they have to *keep* being open to learning."[36] To leverage SDL in order to help employees identify, develop, and enhance the soft and hard skills on a continual basis in the postpandemic marketplace, individuals across almost every industry will need to commit to lifelong learning and develop the essential skills required to remain relevant, vital, and vibrant.

CHAPTER 5

Essential Skills

The global pandemic upended normalcy and dramatically altered the roles and responsibilities of business leaders around the world. Prior to the pandemic, executives focused on sustaining innovation, driving revenue, and remaining competitive. Today and in the postpandemic environment, new priorities have emerged that include controlling costs, resolving unforeseen roadblocks, addressing operational challenges, navigating health and safety concerns, working remotely, and supporting their families through the pandemic. In today's VUCA environment, it is no surprise to learn that 80 percent of the workforce, 92 percent of managers, and 77 percent of senior leaders reported feeling poorly prepared for the future.[1] With the pandemic disorienting feelings of preparedness and altering the fabric of how people live, work, and do just about everything around the world, employers and employees alike need to recognize that "success in the future will require new skills. As the saying goes, "What got you here, won't get you there." "Yesterday's competencies are a starting point, but tomorrow's success will require more and different skills."[2] Reflecting upon the future workforce, Scott Engler declared "The need for critical skills has never been greater. But labor market and talent data suggest many companies have unwittingly built the wrong workforce to drive their future—and continue to do so."[3] To that end, the soft and hard skills dichotomy so prevalent today should be expanded to include essential skills built upon the foundation of self-awareness, self-care, and equanimity.

Kelly Williams, senior vice president and chief human resources officer for the Blue Cross Blue Shield Association, noted self-awareness, when combined with how well people care for themselves mentally and physically in and out of the office, influences everything. In a March 2, 2021, interview Williams said "I would love to see equanimity as a core competency in schools. At the heart of it, it is about being grounded and centered amidst the chaos."[4] As Williams noted, equanimity is a noun that expresses what it means to experience life events with mental calmness, composure, and evenness of temper—especially in difficult situations. While equanimity would have been a useful skill pre-COVID, it is even more so as the world emerges onto the post-COVID period and readjusts to a new normal. Toni Bernhard echoed Williams and described equanimity as "a mental state that enables you to meet life's unpleasant experiences, disappointments, and sad moments with even-tempered calm instead of with aversion."[5] Moreover, equanimity is often associated with a variety of factors such as "improved self-control, objectivity, improved concentration and mental clarity, emotional intelligence and the ability to relate to others and one's self with kindness, acceptance and compassion."[6]

Equanimity would serve leaders well as they look to develop the essential skills required to embrace the ambiguity of the postpandemic world. For example, Harvard Business School Professor Nancy Koehn has suggested management teams stay grounded and "maintain a presence of equanimity to help people make the right decisions and successfully navigate through crisis."[7] In her research on U.S. President Abraham Lincoln's method of leadership, Koehn discovered Lincoln practiced equanimity and relied on the belief that "the higher the stakes, the less likely he was to do anything."[8] Additionally, other researchers have highlighted the necessity of leaders keeping their mind and body in fighting shape. "To consistently deliver results, leaders must maintain their equanimity and establish a routine of self-care."[9] Equanimity is a skill, however, and, as Williams noted, "like all skills, it requires practice."[10]

Such practice should begin in college and serve as a foundation for the graduates who will enter the workforce. With a workforce skilled in the art of equanimity, organizations could rely on their employees to navigate the chaos and embrace the ambiguity of the moment. Unfortunately, three significant trends exist in higher education that overshadow any ability for colleges to implement equanimity as a core competency. First, students are increasingly placing a premium on the job-related benefits of going to college. The portion of incoming freshmen that cited "to be able to get a better job" as a very important reason for attending college reached an all-time high of 87.9 percent in 2012, an increase from 85.9 percent in 2011, and considerably higher than the low of 67.8 percent in 1976. In the minds of today's college students, getting a better job continues to be the most prevalent reason to go to college.[11] Unfortunately, the degree students think will help them secure a high-paying job is often outdated. With an outdated degree in hand, it is no surprise to learn the second trend is the fact that many employers are growing increasingly frustrated by the lack of preparedness of recent college graduates.

A 2016 survey found nearly 90 percent of recent college graduates considered themselves well prepared but only half of hiring managers shared that opinion.[12] This discrepancy between perception and reality is a direct result of the disconnect between higher education institutions and the rest of the community. As Denise Leaser noted "A college degree cannot keep up with the quick rate of change facing most industries. By the time someone graduates, their knowledge is out-of-date."[13] In addition to an outdated degree and a lack of job preparedness, the third trend is the unfortunate reality that while college presents an opportunity for students to challenge themselves in the pursuit of knowledge "habits of the mind are on the decline" as "lifelong learning behaviors associated with academic success are declining among entering college freshmen."[14] As Sophie Ruddock and Ryan Craig observed in an April 23, 2021 article "the higher education system in the United States is antiquated, broken, and failing to provide the right training for jobs in 2021."[15] To help recent college graduates, leaders, managers, and employees at all levels remain relevant, a new model of skill development is required.

There are various models of skill development in existence. The most common model involves the dichotomy of soft and hard skills. Another model stems from a 2018 report from the McKinsey Global Institute identified five distinct skill categories: physical and manual (ranging from truck drivers to nurses), basic cognitive (cashiers and customer service), higher cognitive (critical thinking and complex information processing), social and emotional (traditional "soft skills"), and technological (IT skills, data analysis and research).[16] A third model originated from the Organization of Economic and Co-operation and Development (OECD) that published its 2019 report "Learning Compass 2030: A conceptual learning framework. The OECD distinguished between three different types of skills: cognitive and meta-cognitive skills (critical thinking, creative thinking, learning-to-learn, and self-regulation), social and emotional skills (empathy, self-efficacy, responsibility, and collaboration), and physical and practical skills (using new information and communication technology devices).[17] While these three models, as well as others, helped shape the thinking around skill development prepandemic, the postpandemic environment will demand a new way of thinking. As consulting firm, PWC concluded in its report "Workforce of the future: The competing forces shaping 2030," the face of human capital, employee recruitment, and talent management "no longer mean the same as ten years ago and many of the roles, skills and job titles of tomorrow are unknown to us today."[18] To address the needs of the future, a new paradigm is needed for skill development.

The Embracing Ambiguity Training Program shifts the current emphasis away from the outdated models and, instead, introduces a new paradigm for the postpandemic VUCA environment. There are three characteristics of the essential skills that differentiate them from the soft, hard, or other identified skills emphasized prepandemic. "In the current VUCA world, mindful engagement with the present context by being with one's thoughts without being judgmental is essential."[19] As such, anyone looking to embrace the ambiguity of the postpandemic world needs to practice an essential set of skills designed to encourage self-care, equanimity, and mindfulness. In this context, "mindfulness means maintaining an awareness of our thoughts, emotions, and surrounding environment, through a gentle, nurturing lens. This gives one the tools not only to manage personal life effectively but also enables one to be observant about the impact of their actions."[20]

The first characteristic stems from the etymology of the word "essential," which has its origins from Middle English meaning "in the highest degree." Yes, soft and hard skills are important and will remain so in the postpandemic future. What has been missing for some time now and has created a gap in the learning process of both students and adults is the identification, assessment, and development of essential skills or those "in the highest degree." The debate over soft versus hard skills has only exacerbated this lack of identifying what is essential to succeed. In the postpandemic amplified state of VUCA, one thing is clear, careful attention to new methods and practices will help employers and employees

alike remain relevant. To that end, it is important to recall Karen Martin's phrase "when everything is a priority, nothing is a priority."[21] If all soft and hard skills are a priority then no one skill set is a priority. To successfully embrace the ambiguity of the postpandemic VUCA world, individuals need to identify, assess, and develop their essential skills. Doing so can help them better understand the soft and hard skills they will need as to work toward their next career step.

The second characteristic of these essential skills is that they rest upon the foundation of equanimity. With a future "that has never seemed more nebulous,"[22] equanimity has escalated in relevance for anyone willing to embrace the ambiguity of the postpandemic environment. Equanimity has two characteristics beneficial to anyone willing to set aside time, make it a priority in the life, and practice it: the power of observation and an inner balance. An increase in observation and self-awareness generates the possibility of equanimity. This course of action exemplified how "the greater our equanimity, the greater our ability to prioritize self-care and well-being, and remain balanced as we navigate through the rough waters and gusty winds of change, challenge, and conflict."[23] As Ruth Sutherland, CEO, Samaritans, London, observed "We urgently need to change the status quo and reshape society's priorities to put wellbeing at the heart of everything we do"[24] in the postpandemic world. Recognizing the lack of equanimity in the workplace and "enabling holistic well-being to energize the collective soul we share is the most crucial success in a post-pandemic world."[25] Otherwise, people run the risk of making work the center of their entire life. Doing so can be counter-productive to one's health and happiness. As author Alison Green wrote "centering your life on a job may make you act against your own self-interest and happiness, perhaps by working long hours or accepting behavior you normally wouldn't."[26] Achieving equanimity can help achieve the awareness and balance required to safeguard against such a life situation.

The third characteristic of these essential skills is they prioritize being a person over working as an employee, being over doing, and a life well lived over a job well done. This humanity attribute has two components: asking yourself if your work situation is right for your current life situation and finding balance between life and work. As discussed earlier, the COVID-19 global pandemic served as a splash of cold water on the faces of many people that woke them up to the realization, they were unhappy at their job. Why did it take a global pandemic to wake people up to the realization they were unhappy? Unfortunately, people fail to set aside the time to ask themselves this question as frequently as they should. As Tim Herrera noted in a December 1, 2019 *New York Times* article asking the question "are you doing what you want to be doing?" is one of the toughest questions a person can attempt to answer.[27] For Art Markman, professor of psychology and marketing at the University of Texas at Austin, and author of the book *Bring Your Brain to Work*, people should "evaluate where they think they are in their life about once a year."[28] Failing to engage in the self-care required to ask this important question can often result in an imbalance between life and work. During the pandemic, millions of Americans shifted to working from home and had their working hours bleed into personal hours. Doing so caused many individuals to struggle with separating who they are as a person from what they do for money.[29] Part II of this publication details the Essential Skills training program that can help individuals increase their self-awareness, self-care, and equanimity during the postpandemic period. Organizations can leverage such a program for their employees and create an environment conducive to sustain its future.

PART II

The Training Program

CHAPTER 6

The Embracing Ambiguity Training Program

This Embracing Ambiguity Training Program identifies 10 Essential Skills individuals can develop to help them ask the huge philosophical questions, engage in the necessary self-reflection, and practice the equanimity needed to embrace the ambiguity in a postpandemic world. The 10 skills are as follows:

1. Accept the existence and permanence of chaos.
2. Challenge assumptions to think differently.
3. Connect and empower others.
4. Demonstrate a strong work ethic.
5. Experiment with your life.
6. Get comfortable in uncomfortable situations.
7. Manage stress and anxiety.
8. Recognize the nuance involved with decision making.
9. Remain open to the unfolding of life.
10. Remind yourself destiny is a matter of choice.

These skills were chosen based on three attributes. First, individuals have practiced these skills throughout history and in so doing, provide a tremendous untapped reference point. While so much attention is spent on acquiring soft and hard skills, too little is devoted to understanding the course of human history and the examples provided by others. As author Aldous Huxley quipped "That men do not learn very much from the lessons of history is the most important of all the lessons that history has to teach."[1] These essential skills help us learn from the lessons of history. Second, each skill requires no formal training or related cost. To practice each of these essential skills, no certificate is needed, no online training is required, and no admissions application is demanded. As many researchers like Mike Colagrossi have noted, the future belongs to those who master and accumulate skills, not degrees.[2] Finally, each skill is available to anyone willing to practice. Recognizing these skills as an untapped reference point for everyone regardless of their demographic is not enough; however, as with all skills, these essential ones need to be practiced on a frequent basis. Developing each of these essential skills will require a consistency of application, a reevaluation of personal habits, and a persistent effort applied over time.

The Embracing Ambiguity training program consists of four learning outcomes associated with each of the 10 Essential Skills as shown in Figure 6.1. The chapters in this section consist of two components. The first component explains the skill and related learning outcomes. The second component provides one or more assessments. Upon reviewing each chapter and aspect of the Essential Skills training program, keep the following items in mind:

- There is no order to these 10 essential skills as each one is just as important as the others.
- This is by no means an exhaustive list as other skills can help embrace ambiguity.
- Complete each exercise in order or at random understanding the order is secondary.
- Consider engaging with each exercise frequently to gauge progress.
- Accept the fact that there are no right or wrong answers.
- Stay focused on the goal which is to increase self-awareness.
- Recognize that this program is for workers across all industries, positions, and locations.
- Be sure to set aside plenty of time for each exercise.
- It is perfectly fine to complete a section at a time and then pick up the next one later.

- Maintain a record of answers as doing so will provide an important reflection exercise itself.
- What works for one person may not necessarily work for another.

Essential Skills

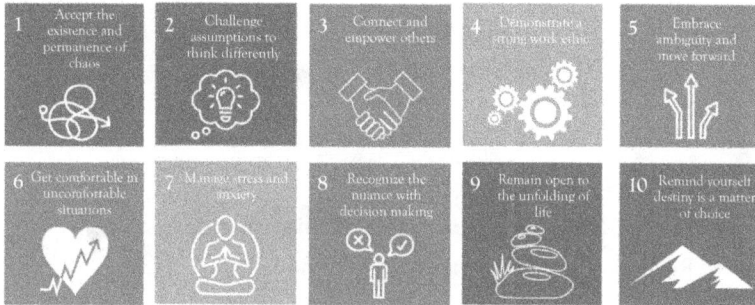

The Essential Skills required to embrace the ambiguity of the post-pandemic economy.

Figure 6.1 The 10 essential skills

Essential Skill 1: *Accept the existence and permanence of chaos.*
Strategies:

- Recognize the unpredictability of external factors.
- Define reality.
- Identify your relationship with chaos.
- Engage in positive uncertainty.

Essential Skill 2: *Challenge assumptions to think differently.*
Strategies:

- Realize the difficulty with being certain.
- Remain aware of the focusing illusion.
- Commit to the process of learning, unlearning, and relearning.
- Differentiate between intuitive and rational thinking.

Essential Skill 3: *Connect and empower others.*
Strategies:

- Practice unbuntu.
- Demonstrate compassion.
- Help others recognize their potential.
- Offer what others need.

Essential Skill 4: *Demonstrate a strong work ethic.*
Strategies:

- Outwork thousands in front of nobody.
- Improve your daily routine to maximize time and effort.
- Reflect upon your relationship with desire.
- Adjust your sails as the winds change.

Essential Skill 5: *Experiment with your life*
Strategies:

- Move forward without a plan.
- Get into the arena of life.
- Go out and meet glory and danger alike.
- Be afraid but do it anyway.

Essential Skill 6: *Get comfortable in uncomfortable situations.*
Strategies:

- Travel outside of life's comfort zone.
- Outgrow your shoes.
- Confront fear and learn how to manage it.
- Learn how to navigate the intersection of fear and grit.

Essential Skill 7: *Manage stress and anxiety.*
Strategies:

- Call upon courage.
- Embrace excitement.

- Remain graceful under pressure.
- Gather strength from distress.

Essential Skill 8: *Understand the role of nuance*
Strategies:

- Assess your decision-making process.
- Decide if you are going to leave, change, or accept your situation.
- Observe your reaction to situations.
- Recognize the space between stimulus and response.

Essential Skill 9: *Remain open to the unfolding of life.*
Strategies:

- Think about your three possible selves.
- Set aside your ego.
- Remain true to yourself.
- Take care of your own grass.

Essential Skill 10: *Remind yourself destiny is a matter of choice.*
Strategies:

- Remain open to the life that is waiting for you.
- Develop your growth mindset.
- Ask yourself how good you want to be.
- Make sure yesterday does not hold you back from tomorrow.

In March 2021, Google opened enrollment for individuals to earn Google Career Certificates in various IT fields. Such a move was Google's latest to help "build an economy that is more inclusive and equitable."[3] According to Sundar Pichai, CEO of Google and Alphabet "efforts such as Google's will remain important in the postpandemic world, but much more is needed." Emphasizing the 10 Essential Skills can help fill the tremendous gap in the marketplace. As Patrick Tucker, technology editor at Defense One and author of *The Naked Future*, observed: "we cannot

prepare coming generations the same way we prepared previous generations to be factory workers. The great thinkers of the 21st century will
understand more about how they process knowledge, assess experiences,
and develop their self than any student in any previous generation."[4] BRG
Managing Director Randy Moon echoed Tucker's comment and said, "We
are in a time of unprecedented uncertainty and the great leaders of this era
will be those who find opportunities in ambiguity, who face uncertainty
with the belief that the magic happens in the grey areas."[5] As former CEO
Jean Hoffman said reflecting upon her career "one of the keys to success
is, you have to be comfortable making decisions in ambiguous situations
and learn from those decisions and get better each day. Those mistakes
are part of the success. They really aren't mistakes."[6] Getting comfortable
making decisions in ambiguous situations; however, benefits those who
can openly admit how uncertainty makes them uncomfortable and anxious. Such admission "removes some of the pressure that may be keeping
one from thinking about what to do about the situations prompting these
emotions in the first place."[7]

In addition to getting comfortable with ambiguity, leaders looking to succeed in the postpandemic marketplace will need to optimize
human development to drive employee engagement and productivity
for a radically different environment in order to create a high-perfor-
mance workplace. In January 2021 and reflecting upon what organizations need to do to succeed post pandemic, researchers from Gallup
noted "The most effective organizations will support and amplify human
development that, in turn, will allow more to be done with less as its
staff becomes highly developed, adaptable, and agile."[8] This concept of
human development has been around for some time but has taken on
new meaning post pandemic as organizations struggle to find both the
quantity and quality of employees needed. Back in 2015, Geoff Colvin
wrote *Humans Are Underrated: What High Achievers Know that Brilliant
Machines Never Will* and emphasized the need for human development.
For Colvin, workers need to "become champions at the skills of human
interaction-empathy above all, social sensitivity, collaboration, storytelling, solving problems together, and building relationships."[9] Pricewater-
houseCoopers (PwC) made a similar observation that same year when
it published a white paper stating "self-awareness involves being clear

on personal values, understanding your strengths and weaknesses, and being cognizant of one's impact on others."[10] Human development is at the core of the Essential Skills included in this Embracing Ambiguity training program. The questions, assessments, and exercises included in this publication can help one identify their personal values, understand the frequency by which they practice each Essential Skill, and provide a blueprint on things to work on moving forward. With that in mind, this publication now turns its attention to the 10 Essential Skills and related assessments of the Embracing Ambiguity training program in the post-pandemic VUCA world.

CHAPTER 7

Essential Skill 1: Accept the Existence and Permanence of Chaos

To embrace the ambiguity of a postpandemic world, the first essential skill to develop is to accept the existence and permanence of chaos. Such a skill provides the necessary perspective if one wants to maintain a macro perspective of life and work in the postpandemic world. Just as the plane flying at 35,000 feet provides the perspective of the entire landscape, so too does an understanding of the permanence of chaos. If all one does is walk upon the ground with their head down, it is difficult to look up and start to comprehend the complexity of the universe. While it is easy to fall prey to the cognitive bias of presentism and believe the present is far more chaotic than any previous period, rest assured previous generations had similar thoughts. For example, as far back as 350 BC, when Plato wrote *Phaedrus*, his protagonist, Socrates, expresses disdain for writing. Writing, Socrates feared, would allow people to stop relying upon their memory, become forgetful, and instead, rely on the written word as opposed to oral history. The principle means of communication at the time, emerging out of necessity, was a long chain of oral storytelling.[1] It was the encounter with modernity, the use of writing, that eliminated this long chain of oral storytelling in many cultures. As Tammy Hepps noted "The irony that Socrates' sentiments would have been forgotten had not his students put his disdain for the written word into written words points to the complicated relationship between the two."[2] And therein lies the intersection of two dynamics: oral history and writing, creating chaos over 2000 years ago. To accept the existence and permanence of chaos, history provides evidence of the four strategies included in this section of the training program: recognize the unpredictability of external factors, define reality, identify your relationship with chaos, and engage in positive uncertainty.

The first strategy to practice the essential skill of accepting the existence and permanence of chaos is to recognize the unpredictability of external factors. In a January 18, 2021 *Psyche* article, "The mathematical case against blaming people for their misfortune," David Kinney highlights the role of complexity science, specifically, computational complexity theory, in explaining the misfortunes that befall some people. Putting aside any political, social, moral, or economic reasoning, Kinney concluded "mathematically that there are hard limits on our capacity to make accurate and precise calculations of risk."[3] For example, Kinney stated how difficult it is to predict future events. As a result of such a high level of uncertainty, "it is unfair to blame people with good intentions who end up worse off because of unforeseen circumstances. This leads to the conclusion that compassion, not blame, is the appropriate attitude towards those who act in good faith but whose bets in life don't pay off."[4] A brief glimpse into four external factors involved with the New York taxi industry serves as an illustration.

- **Industry leaders:** For more than a decade, New York taxi industry leaders became rich by creating a bubble in the market for the city permits, known as medallions, that allow people to own and operate cabs.
- **Government officials:** An investigation by *The New York Times* found that government officials stood by as industry leaders artificially inflated medallion prices and channeled immigrant drivers into loans they could not afford to purchase the permits. The leaders reaped hundreds of millions of dollars before the bubble burst, wiping out thousands of buyers mired in debt.[5]
- **Competition:** Although New York City caps the number of yellow cabs at just over 13,600, it does not limit the number of drivers for Uber, Lyft, or other services. (It does, unlike most U.S. cities, require that ride-share drivers be licensed by the Taxi and Limousine Commission.) The lack of regulation led to rapid growth as the number of cars available via ride

share mobile apps skyrocketed from 105 in 2011, to 20,000 in 2015, and over 60,000 in 2018.[6]

- **Market response:** With the number of medallions fixed, prices generally rose, peaking in 2014 at over $1 million— well outside the budget of many drivers, but good news for medallion owners who sometimes borrowed against them. Since then, though, prices have fallen sharply, as competition from ride-hailing services intensified. In 2016, lenders foreclosed on 23 medallions. That number grew to 46 in 2017 and skyrocketed to 494 in 2018. Additionally, the precipitous decline of the yellow cab business led to a record 510 foreclosures of taxi medallion-backed loans in 2019.[7]

Sadly, the unpredictability of external factors was so overwhelming in 2018. Six New York City taxi drivers committed suicide.[8] Noting our limited ability to associate multiple characteristics of today's complex world, Kinney noted "No matter how smart we think we are, there is a hard limit on what we can know, and we could easily end up on the losing end of a big bet. We owe it to ourselves, and others, to build a more compassionate world."[9]

Learning how to deal with reality is another strategy to practice the essential skill of accepting the existence and permanence of chaos. As American writer Alex Haley noted "Either you deal with what is the reality, or you can be sure that the reality is going to deal with you." After facing the reality that he did not belong in college, Haley dropped out and at his father's suggestion joined the Coast Guard and enlisted as a mess attendant. Later, he was promoted to the rate of petty officer third-class in the rating of steward, one of the few ratings open to African Americans at that time. It was during his service in the Pacific theater of operations that Haley taught himself the craft of writing stories. During his enlistment, other sailors often paid him to write love letters to their girlfriends. He said that the greatest enemy he and his crew faced during their long voyages was not the Japanese forces but rather boredom.

After World War II, Haley petitioned the U.S. Coast Guard to allow him to transfer into the field of journalism. By 1949, he had become a petty officer first-class in the rating of journalist. He later advanced to chief petty officer and held this grade until his retirement from the Coast Guard in 1959. He was the first chief journalist in the Coast Guard, the rating having been expressly created for him in recognition of his literary ability. Haley would go on to author the best-selling 1976 book *Roots: The Saga of an American Family* and coauthored *The Autobiography of Malcolm X*.[10] In *Roots*, the Pulitzer Prize-winning author chronicled his ancestors' origins in Africa and their passage from slavery to freedom in America. In short, Haley dealt with reality by writing about it.

Upon reflecting on his career, Haley said, "I was a sailor, I was a cook and this and that, and it might be said I was bootstrapped up to being a writer."[11] As a testament to his relationship with reality, Haley went further and said, "the real bootstrapping had been done earlier by his father, who rose from humble beginnings to earn a graduate degree in agriculture and went on to teach in Southern colleges."[12] By dealing with reality in an honest manner, Haley accepted the existence of the chaos, embraced the ambiguity of his day, and learned how to navigate his life and career in order to leave a permanent mark on American culture.

A third strategy to practice the essential skill of accepting the existence and permanence of chaos is to identify one's relationship with it. This strategy involves what Swiss psychiatrist and psychoanalyst Carl Jung wrote about in one of his over 1,600 letters he penned during his lifetime. Jung wrote about vision and the need to see clearly. Commenting on vision, Jung suggested that "vision will become clear only when you can look in your own heart. Without, everything seems discordant; only within does it coalesce into unity. Who looks outside dreams, who looks inside awakes."[13] This ability to look inside to awaken is critical for anyone who wants to identify their relationship with chaos. For those who take on a new role filled with disruption, it is imperative they identify their relationship with chaos as it is a precursor to success. One such example who serves as a reference here is the accomplished German conductor, Kurt Masur.

Masur directed many of the principal orchestras of his era including the New York Philharmonic. When Masur arrived in New York, he inherited an orchestra that needed to be reengineered from its foundation. The once famed orchestra "had devolved into a mess of a lackluster group, that was critically skewered, internally contentious and lacked clear artistic vision."[14] To add to the chaos into which he stepped, "Audiences were disenchanted. The players had long been unhappy; recording engagements were hard to come by, and radio broadcasts were nonexistent. Symphonic music was becoming less important to the culture of New York."[15] Masur understood his relationship with chaos and believed he could bring order, progress, and stability where it was needed most. His upbringing paved the way. Masur's father was an engineer and insisted his son study to become an electrician. Fortunately, young Masur also studied music training as a pianist, organist, cellist, and percussionist.

Wanting to make music his calling, he entered the National Music School in Breslau. Unfortunately, by the time he was 16, an inoperable tendon injury in his right hand had made performing musical instruments impossible. With a commitment to make music his life, Masur adjusted to the chaos of having the use of one hand and decided to pivot and concentrate on conducting. As a result of the hand condition, Masur conducted without a baton throughout his career. As Masur recalled in an interview, it was during this time in his early life that he said to himself "I have to be a conductor. I have to make music otherwise I die."[16] Losing his ability to use one hand as a conductor was chaotic but Masur looked inside of himself to have a better understanding of how to succeed. He would go on to be known for a disciplined and strict approach to conducting. When people would point to the wonder of him as a one-arm conductor Masur would deflect the attention and said "I don't want to be called a wonder. The wonder is the music."[17] Masur is just one of the many examples of people who had to face reality and identify their relationship with chaos to embrace the ambiguity of their life situation. As Masur's story demonstrated, life will most likely not go according to plan. So, what do you do then? For Masur, he accepted the chaos, embraced the ambiguity of being a one arm conductor, and found a way forward.

Engaging in positive uncertainty is another strategy to practice the essential skill of accepting the existence and permanence of chaos. Today is uncertain. Tomorrow is uncertain. Next month is uncertain. In short, life is uncertain. Despite this level of uncertainty, some people find a way to engage in what is known as positive uncertainty. Reflecting upon personal tragedies he experienced, actor Mark Ruffalo said "Those experiences helped me realize the fallibility of human beings and left me with a feeling that I am not that certain about anything. None of us know the ending of the story. All of us are walking around with an enormous amount of uncertainty."[18]

Remember, the U in VUCA refers to Uncertainty. In the post-pandemic world, the level of uncertainty is certain to increase! In *The Chaos Theory of Careers: A New Perspective on Working in the Twenty-First Century*, authors Robert Pryor and Jim Bright noted "uncertainty reveals limitation and limitation signals vulnerability but it also suggests there may be potentials within us and possibilities around us of which we may be currently unaware."[19] These possibilities await us, Pryor and Bright believe, if we "have the courage to run the gauntlet of uncertainty; that is, to risk vulnerability and failure in the quest for opportunity and achievement."[20] To deal with positive uncertainty, which involves complexity, change, and chance, researcher H. B. Gelatt identified four major paradoxes that successful people who have navigated the chaos understand as they move forward in their career decision-making process:

- Be focused and flexible about what you want.
- Be aware and wary about what you know.
- Be objective and optimistic about what you believe.
- Be practical and magical about what you do.

These four paradoxes can be used to embrace the ambiguity of a post-pandemic world that will continue to be VUCA. Positive uncertainty is compatible with the new science and beliefs of today's society and incompatible with yesterday's decision dogma. It involves ambiguity and paradox because the future is full of ambiguity and paradox. In the future, it will help to realize that one does not know some things, cannot always see what is coming, and frequently will not be able to control it. Successful people remain positive amidst the uncertainty to create options as it allows them to act when one is uncertain about what they are doing. In a July 2015 article published in *Forbes* entitled "*Why Embracing Uncertainty Is Critical to Your Success*," Margie Warrell emphasized the need to "continually assess whether we are letting our fear of the unknown keep us from taking the actions to move us forward." If fear is holding people back, Warrell suggested, then she recommended reflecting upon the question "what you would do if you were not afraid of failing? The first answer that pops into your head will point you in a direction you need to go, albeit an uncertain one."[21] To step into the unknown, one will need to be comfortable with both taking a risk and the uncertainty involved with the situation. As you consider using the strategy of engaging in positive uncertainty to practice the essential skill of accepting the permanence of chaos, remind yourself of the axiom "nothing worthwhile has ever been accomplished with a guarantee of success." Embracing the ambiguity of a postpandemic world requires one to move forward without any guarantee of success. As Warrell noted, "Too often we interpret our failure's as permanent inadequacies on our part and use them as an excuse to stick to what we know we're good at."[22] Positive uncertainly allows one the ability to move forward going from one failure to another while engaging in the self-reflection required to learn from each one as you embrace the ambiguity of a postpandemic world.

The four strategies related to the essential skill of accepting the existence and permanence of chaos are as follows: recognize the unpredictability of external factors, define reality, identify your relationship with chaos, and engage in positive uncertainty. This first skill may be challenging for you to develop. Many people struggle to accept the permanence of chaos or fail to differentiate between the existence of chaos and their ability to not engage in it. This first essential skill is about acceptance. The postpandemic world will continue to be VUCA. The more individuals and organizations can accept this fact, the better prepared they can be. This Embracing Ambiguity training program provides a wide spectrum of self-assessments to complete. The following assessments are designed to engage in the individual in the self-care, self-awareness, and equanimity needed to embrace the ambiguity of the postpandemic VUCA world. Armed with a better sense of self, the individual can then practice the strategies outlined here. That is what Bob Miglani did. In his 2013 publication *Embrace the Chaos: How India Taught Me to Stop Overthinking and Start Living*, Miglani increased his self-awareness, grew to accept the permanence of chaos, and in so doing learned the power of letting go. He stopped trying to control the chaos and instead, started focusing on what was in his control—his actions, words, and thoughts. Remember, the only thing within anyone's control is how they react to a situation, how they think, and their work ethic. That's it/Nothing more. People may want to be in control of more, but the harsh reality is one only controls their reaction, thoughts, and work ethic. Embracing the chaos, according to Miglani, allows people to travel down "paths they never have walked on, and it brings out strengths they never knew existed inside of them."[23] This chapter provided numerous examples of how individuals who accepted the existence and permanence of chaos. These lessons are available to anyone willing to engage in the self-reflection, self-awareness, and self-care required to apply such experiences to the postpandemic world. This essential skill of accepting the existence and permanence of chaos has been around for a long-time and will continue to serve as a viable option for those looking to embrace the ambiguity of the years ahead. Accepting the existence and permanence of chaos can also help one practice the next essential skill of challenging assumptions to think differently.

Assessment: Open-Ended Questions

- How often do you recognize the unpredictability of external factors?
- Throughout your career, can you identify five external factors that proved to be unpredictable and that had a significant impact on your job, organization, or industry?
- What external factors have impacted your career trajectory?
- How has your response been to external factors?
- Have you helped others respond to external factors?
- How do you react, or what do you think, when you encounter a poor person?
- Are you so certain of their life situation that you can blame their poverty solely on them?
- Do you demonstrate compassion toward those less fortunate?
- How often do you define reality?
- How do you reconcile your definition of reality with someone else's view?

- How would you define reality know for your organization?
- How does your version of reality compare to others in your organization?
- How often does your senior leadership define reality?
- What are you doing to guard against your own biases when defining reality?
- How often do you deal with reality?
- How do you respond to someone whose reality differs from your own?

Exercise: Plan A, B, C ....

Write one specific goal here: _____

Directions: While some people will tell you "There is no plan B," the reality is life often provides viable alternatives to Plan A that you never even considered. To help process your thinking around a specific goal, write down as many plans, or strategies, you can take to achieve the goal you listed on the above line. Remember, there are 26 letters to the alphabet. This exercise is challenging you to write down at least five different plans to achieve your goal. How many can you identify?

Plan A

Plan B

Plan C

Plan D

Plan E

Assessment: Frequency Related to Chaos

Directions: For each of the following statements, use the following Likert scale to determine your frequency: never, rarely, sometimes, often, always. Write your answer next to each statement. How often have you ...

1. Decided on a course of action but the result was something you had never considered?
2. Allowed fear to prevent you from doing something important in your life?
3. Achieved a goal but then realized you wanted something else instead?
4. Benefitted from not getting something you wanted?
5. Viewed a situation one way but find out someone else sees it a completely different way?
6. Experienced an unplanned event that had a big impact on your life?
7. Found it an advantage not to know something?
8. Lived through a significant experience that changed your life in some way?
9. Been in either the right or wrong place at the right or wrong time?
10. Followed your instincts or intuition?
11. Relied on information when making a decision only to discover later that it was incorrect?
12. Distorted reality to yourself or to others?
13. Move forward without having a specific plan in mind?
14. Set a clear goal and discovered a better one along the way?
15. Demonstrated irrational behavior?
16. Been told something personal about yourself, of which you were completely unaware?
17. Did you act or speak before thinking?
18. Have you ever made a small mistake that resulted in a big problem later on down the line?
19. Have things occurred in your life that you never thought would have been possible?
20. Allowed yourself to realize impossibly terrible things were possible, but so too are impossibly wonderful things possible.

Select the appropriate number of times you answered often or always:

A. 15 or more often or always
B. 10–14 often or always
C. 5–9 often or always
D. 0–4 often or always

A = you have a strong awareness of just how chaotic life is.

B = you have a developing sense of the chaos of life around you.

C = you sporadically accept the chaos of life.

D = you have yet to embrace the chaos around you.

Assessment: Use of Positive Uncertainty

Directions: Reflect upon a recent time-period and answer the following questions to understand your relationship with the four paradoxes of positive uncertainty. Choose from any of the following periods of time:

- The last 24 hours
- The last week
- The last two weeks
- The last month

During the last _____ how often did you....

- Remain focused and flexible about what you wanted?
- Stay aware yet wary about what you know?
- Remain objective and optimistic about what you believed?
- Stay practical yet magical about what you did?
- What are some of the challenges involved with remaining focused and flexible, aware, and wary, objective and optimistic, and practical and magical?
- How often do you allow yourself to be vulnerable amidst uncertainty?
- Have you allowed uncertainty ...
    o ... To reveal something more hopeful?
    o To suggest there lies within you some untapped potential?
    o To challenge you to think differently?
    o To realize you have the courage required to move forward anyway?
    o To risk vulnerability and failure in the quest for opportunity and achievement.
- How often do you engage in positive uncertainty?

CHAPTER 8

Essential Skill 2: Challenge Assumptions to Think Differently

Challenging assumptions to help you think differently is the second essential skill to develop for those interested in embracing the ambiguity of a postpandemic world. The move from the office to the home for millions in March 2020 at the onset of the pandemic challenged managers to think differently. With such a dramatic move, almost overnight, managers faced the unprecedented task of challenging their assumptions about how their employees would get their work done while balancing the new needs of remaining at home. Nina Bartmann, Senior Behavioral Researcher, Center for Advanced Hindsight at Duke University noted the importance of "establishing work-life boundaries when the home is the new office so that people can maintain mental wellbeing."[1] To that end, leaders and managers need to remind themselves to develop, and prioritize the two key traits of trust and compassion. According to Ben Pring, Director of Cognizant's Center for the Future of Work, with employees performing their work out of site, the unprecedented times of the pandemic called for employers to use a "more trusting, compassionate, and human approach to leadership as it will be vital in helping teams get through things unscathed."[2] But for many micromanagers, who held on to the archaic belief that employees only work when they are in the office, challenging their assumptions and thinking differently proved a herculean task.

Recent research prior to the pandemic found that "a perceived loss of control and a sense of being taken advantage of, may be experienced by a manager as employees disappear from the manager's daily gaze."[3] The micromanager's obsession with seeing an employee sitting at their office desk, as opposed to trusting they are working at home, is problematic, causes unnecessary stress on the culture, and can negatively impact an employee's mental wellbeing. As researchers noted, "When such doubts creep in, managers can start to develop an unreasonable expectation that those team members be available all the time, ultimately disrupting their work-home balance and causing more job stress."[4] To challenge assumptions and think differently, history provides evidence of the four strategies included in this section of the training program: realize the difficulty with being certain, remain aware of the focusing illusion, commit to the process of learning, unlearning, and relearning, and differentiate between intuitive and rational thinking.

The first strategy to practice the essential skill of challenging assumptions to think differently is to realize the difficulty with being certain. Plans are made and then changed. Directions are outlined and then altered. Schedules are created and then altered. The uncertainty of life might be perhaps the most certain aspect of living there is. Learning to deal with uncertainty is a fundamental element involved with embracing the ambiguity in a postpandemic world. Commenting on the uncertainty of life during the COVID-19 pandemic, Steven Petrow observed in *The New York Times,* "Sometimes hope lies in the unknown."[5] This can be especially prescient when times are overwhelmingly hard and scary, and the immediate future remains bleak. But within that "uncertainty and unpredictability—suddenly and surprisingly—are where there's an opening for hope."[6] When sharing his secret to happiness, the great philosopher Jiddu Krishnamurti said, "Do you want to know what my secret is? I don't mind what happens."[7] How many times have you said to yourself "I don't mind what happens?" Be honest. You may have said "I don't mind what happens" aloud to others or to yourself but is that how you feel? Reflecting upon your answer to that question helps you increase your self-awareness as it relates to a need to be certain. Truth be told, most people do mind what happens.

Most people, however, mind what happens, as Allison Carmen reminded readers in a *Psychology Today* article, because of their obligations to family, self, and other aspects of their lives. "We want to make sure that the things we want to happen do happen,"[8] Carmen wrote, and "that is exactly where our need for certainty begins. We want to know what will happen next so we could rest in the moment knowing everything will be okay."[9] If the pandemic taught us anything it is that everything may not be okay, and we must find a way forward amidst the ambiguity. Holding onto certainty, or at least believing it is on the horizon and within grasp, has consequences to consider. For example, Ted Cadsby acknowledged "the need to be certain gets in the way of accuracy when it comes to problems with multiple, interwoven causal factors that are difficult to unbundle."[10] In a postpandemic world where embracing ambiguity will remain a constant, it is imperative to understand the exploration, perspectives, and analysis required to propose potential explanations prior to reaching any level of certainty. As Cadsby noted, "many complex problems can only be tackled with experimentation because they do not converge to definitive solutions."[11]

When one maintains the belief that being certain is feasible, or even a viable strategy to use in a postpandemic world, it is important to recall the work of Philip Tetlock in *Expert Political Judgment: How Good Is It? How Can We Know?* where he concluded "the average expert was found to be only slightly more accurate than a dart-throwing chimpanzee. Many experts would have done better if they had made random guesses."[12] So much for being certain! Tetlock made his conclusion after studying over 82,000 predictions from 284 people who made their living "commenting or offering advice on political and economic trends" over a 20-year period. In his November 28, 2005, *New Yorker* review of Tetlock's book, Louis Menand discounted the level of certainty that exists among experts and wrote "people appearing as experts in the press, advise governments and businesses, and participate in punditry roundtables—are no better than the rest of us. When they are wrong, they are rarely held accountable, and they rarely admit it."[13]

Remaining aware of the focusing illusion is another strategy to practice the essential skill of challenging assumptions to think differently. The focusing illusion is also known as the focusing effect and is a cognitive bias that occurs when people place too much importance on one aspect of an event, causing an error in accurately predicting the utility of a future outcome. In his 2011 book, *Thinking Fast and Slow*, the 2002 Nobel Prize recipient in Economics, Daniel Kahneman, discussed his concept of the focusing illusion and defined it as meaning "Nothing in life is as important as you think it is while you are thinking about it."[14] To identify the focusing illusion one must think hard and, as Kahneman noted, since people "are not accustomed to thinking hard, they are often content to trust a plausible judgment that quickly comes to mind."[15] Dr. Louis Tay applied the focusing illusion to the COVID-19 pandemic in a blog post and discussed other factors people need to do to stay healthy and safe, in addition to the vaccination. For example, yes, vaccinations are important, but so too are seatbelts in cars.[16] Believing the COVID-19 vaccination is all one needs to be safe during the pandemic, at the expense of ignoring other safety protocols, is an example of the focusing illusion. When Kahneman applied the focusing illusion to education, he made the following observation: "Education is an important determinant of income—one of the most important—but it is less important than most people think."[17] Perhaps, nowhere is the focusing illusion more apparent than in the discussion between one's college major and future earnings income potential.

Evidence suggests little correlation between one's level of education or academic major and long-term income potential. "In one recent survey over 90 percent of employers agree that a candidate's demonstrated capacity to think critically, communicate clearly, and solve complex problems is more important than their undergraduate major."[18] Daniel Hamermesh of the University of Texas concluded that "Perceptions of the variations in economic success among graduates in different majors are exaggerated."[19] There are simply too many other factors, to consider when trying to calculate a return on investment at the level of one's academic major in college. According to Hamermesh, "Our results imply that given a student's ability, achievement and effort, their earnings do not vary all that greatly with the choice of undergraduate major."[20] Focusing solely on education prevents the consideration of the myriad of other factors that determine income. For example, Angela Duckworth has found "grit, the tendency to sustain interest in and effort toward very long-term goals, is the single greatest factor determining your future success."[21] Falling into the focusing illusion trap would have one believe one degree is better to have than another. Nothing could be further from the truth.

Another strategy to practice the essential skill of challenging assumptions to think differently is to commit to the process of learning, unlearning, and relearning. In a small but impactful publication entitled *The Measure of Our Success: A Letter to My Children and Yours*, Marian Wright Edelman, American activist and founder of the Children's Defense Fund, wrote "My father stressed education. My parents taught us that education and knowledge were an individual's source of strength."[22] To emphasize what her father stressed, Edelman challenged readers to "never stop learning and improving your mind or you are going to get left behind. The world is changing like a kaleidoscope right before our eyes."[23] Edelman made that observation decades ago when the pace of change moved at a glacial speed compared to the disruption found in today's world. In a world where today's students will have job not yet created using technologies not yet invented to solve problems not yet identified, it is an absolute imperative that individuals across all industries demonstrate a commitment to being a life-long learner. In the postpandemic marketplace remember the virus did not transform society as much as it did accelerate the change already underway in a volatile, uncertain, complex, and ambiguous (VUCA) world. With disruptive technologies altering entire industries, causing drastic change in how people work, communicate, live, and just do about everything else, the number of jobs where people can simply turn up and be told how to do the job and be well paid for it is diminishing rapidly. John Howkins author of *The Creative Economy* noted "We need now to go on learning throughout our lives. When somebody stops learning, now it is like they have stopped thinking, or at least being creative."[24]

Futurist and best-selling author, Alvin Toffler echoed similar thoughts when reflecting on how individuals can succeed in a world marked by constant disruption and concluded "the illiterate of the 21st century will not be those who cannot read and write, but those who cannot learn, unlearn, and relearn."[25] Committing to the process of learning, unlearning, and relearning in the postpandemic world, however, can be a herculean challenge for many people. As American inventor and businessman Charles Kettering quipped, "People are very open-minded about new things—as long as they're exactly like the old ones."[26] This lack of connecting, developing, or using a new idea is also known as cognitive inertia. Cognitive inertia refers to the tendency for beliefs or sets of beliefs to endure once formed. The phrase "we've always done it this way", and any resistance to change, is a common adage illustrating cognitive inertia. The inclination to rely on familiar assumptions and exhibit a reluctance and/or inability to revise those assumptions, even when the evidence supporting them no longer exists or when other evidence would question their accuracy, presents a unique challenge to those looking to change a situation.

Differentiating between intuitive and rational thinking is another strategy to practice the essential skill of challenging assumptions to think differently. Thinking about thinking is hard work. So too are the other essential skills. Remember, the essential skills require substantial self-awareness, reflection, and frequency of practice. Soft skills will help individuals get along with others and hard skills will allow people to complete certain tasks. But Essential Skills will allow one to gain the self-knowledge required to embrace the ambiguity of the postpandemic world. For example, just getting through the day in the postpandemic world can be challenging enough for most people. In the postpandemic world, differentiating between intuitive and rational thinking, also known as thinking hard, will be a requirement for anyone who wants to remain relevant. Making decisions in the postpandemic and VUCA world requires a keen mind that understands the value, utility, and purpose of intuitive and rational thinking. Knowing what to think will remain important, but due to the continued disruption of the global marketplace, recognizing how to think will be just as valuable. When provided the time and resources to think things through, humans can be quite rational, but when constrained by time quick, gut-feeling decisions are often relied upon. How often are you aware of your decision-making process?

In his 2011 book *Thinking, Fast and Slow*, psychologist and Nobel laureate Daniel Kahneman explains the so-called dual-process theory of decision making for lay audiences. According to dual-process theory, intuitive thinking is fast, while rational thinking is slow. To identify the type of thinking utilized to solve a problem, researchers often use reaction time to determine whether a participant in their experiment is using an intuitive or rational approach. Going with one's gut, however, and having a short reaction time, is not necessarily bad. Social psychologist Anthony Evans has argued "a fast reaction time can correlate with either an intuitive or a rational decision process, depending on the particular task."[27] For example, humans have evolved some effective intuitions that usually lead to very quick—and reasonably accurate—judgments, at least in the social realm. Likewise, taking the time to make a rational decision can lead us to what psychologists call "paralysis by analysis." That is, people are unable to decide in real time because they are bogged down by slow reasoning processes. Over the years, researchers have created a variety of tests to help people better understand the level of their intuitive thinking compared to rational decision making.

In 1998, researchers Anthony Greenwald, Debbie McGhee, and Jordan Schwartz created one such test when they introduced the Implicit Association Test (IAT). The IAT measures the milliseconds it takes to connect pairs of ideas. According to the IAT's website, the instrument "measures attitudes and beliefs that people may be unwilling or unable to report and may be especially interesting if it shows you have an implicit attitude you did not know about."[28] The IAT is particularly helpful in identifying the associations people make with gender or race. "For example, you may believe that women and men should be equally associated with science, but your automatic associations could show that you (like many others) associate men with science more than you associate women with science."[29] In his 2005 book *Blink: The Power of Thinking Without Thinking*, Malcolm Gladwell described how upset he was when his unconscious association with Caucasian-European was "good" and his association with African American was "bad"—even though Gladwell himself is half-black![30] Such an experience taught Gladwell "to disregard his first impressions of people and to take time to know them before passing any judgement."[31] In other words, to improve his ability to think Gladwell started to emphasize rational over intuitive thinking. But those associations Gladwell had, many of them were unconscious and we all have them to some degree.[32]

The four strategies related to the essential skill of challenging assumptions to think differently are as follows: realize the difficulty with being certain; remain aware of the focusing illusion, commit to the process of learning, unlearning, and relearning; and differentiate between intuitive and rational thinking. On May 27, 2021, *New York Times* columnist David Brooks discussed the transition societies are undergoing from mandating masks to taking off the physical masks as vaccination rates rise. Brooks wrote that "it seems important that we take off the psychological masks as well."[33] Referencing the difficultly people have with thinking differently, Brooks concluded that one certainty he has learned over his lifetime is that "More lives are wrecked by the slow and frigid death of emotional closeness than by the short and hot risks of emotional openness."[34] In the postpandemic world, embracing the ambiguity will require the challenging of assumptions in parallel with thinking hard. With new global trends disrupting the marketplace for almost every industry, those who wish to remain vibrant, relevant, and vital will need to practice this essential skill of thinking differently on a frequent basis. This chapter provided numerous examples of how individuals who challenged their assumptions to think differently. These lessons are available to anyone willing to engage in the self-reflection, self-awareness, and self-care required to apply such experiences to the postpandemic world. This essential skill of challenging assumption to think differently has been around for a long-time and will continue to serve as a viable option for those looking to embrace the ambiguity of the years ahead. Challenging assumptions to think differently can also help one practice the next essential skill of connecting with and empowering others.

Assessment: Open-Ended Questions

- During the last month how often have the following happened?
  o Your made plans but needed to change them.
  o Someone made plans with you, but they needed to change them.
  o You were provided directions but then they were altered.
  o You had a schedule, but it needed to be changed for whatever reason.
- On a scale of 1 (lowest) to 10 (highest) how comfortable are you with uncertainty? For example, a score of 9 would suggest you are rather comfortable with a high level of uncertainty.
- Have you ever found hope in uncertainty?
- Have you even considered that hope exists in uncertainty?
- How often do you mind what happens?
- How does it make you feel when you are uncertain about someone you love?

- How did you process the uncertainty you experienced during the pandemic?
- What lessons can you learn from how you processed uncertainty during the pandemic?
- How often did you say to yourself (or perhaps to others) that you want things to go back to "normal" after the pandemic?
- Why do you think you/others held on to the belief of normalcy in a postpandemic world?
- Have you ever thought about how your need to be certain overshadowed any hope of experimentation to explore, wonder, or assess a situation?
- Have you made a decision based on some expert advice only to find out later it was wrong?
- Have you tried to let go of your need to be certain? If not, why do you think it is so difficult for you to do so?
- Have you engaged in the focusing illusion?
- Why do you think people place such a strong emphasis on that which is right in front of them?
- How do you help yourself gain the necessary perspective required to see the big picture?
- How often do you stress education as a critical component of succeeding in a postpandemic world?
- What have you done lately to improve your mind?
- How has your learning changed during the pandemic?
- Do you understand how the pandemic accelerated change around the world?
- Have you experienced first-hand the way the pandemic changed our world?
- How often have you told yourself that the world is changing too fast, and you are unable to keep up with it? If you have, why do you think that is?
- Do you agree with Toffler in that the "illiterate of the 21st century will not be those who cannot read and write, but those who cannot learn, unlearn, and relearn?"
- Why do you think, as Charles Kettering noted "People are very open-minded about new things—as long as they're exactly like the old ones?"

Exercise: Focusing Illusion

- Respond to the following definition of the focusing illusion by applying this explanation to a recent situation in your life.

Nothing in life is quite as important as you think it is while you are thinking about it and as merely thinking about something will make you exaggerate its importance in your life.

While there are dozens of cognitive biases to consider, how do you think the following six impact one's focusing illusion?

- Framing Effect—You can draw radically different conclusions from the same information, depending on how it is presented.
- IKEA Effect—You place a disproportionately higher value on things you personally create or contribute to.
- Mere Exposure Effect—Increased favorability toward things merely because you are familiar with them.
- Zero Risk Bias—Prefer reducing a small risk to zero over a greater reduction in a larger risk.
- Illusory Correlation Bias—Inaccurately seeing a cause/effect relationship toward random events.
- Hindsight Bias—Tendency to filter the memory of past events through present knowledge ("I knew it all along" distortion).

Assessment: Differentiating Between Intuitive and Rational Thinking

Directions: For this assessment select a situation in your life and choose one from each of the following pairs as to how you responded. This is situational so be specific as doing so will help you better identify your ability to differentiate between intuitive and rational thinking. Select A or B from each pair. Perhaps use a separate sheet of paper should you be interested in completing this assessment multiple times for different situations.

In this situation did you …

A. Create solutions to the problem by identifying the causes of irregularities.
B. Generate unconventional ideas.
A. Define the various components involved with multiple ideas for solutions and then conduct the necessary fact-based analysis to select one.
B. Involve feelings and emotions in the assessment process of choosing among multiple options for solutions.
A. Carefully estimate the costs and benefits associated with each alternative solution to the problem.
B. Reject one or more of the potential solutions based on emotions.
A. Rely on external information from different sources.
B. Use both external information and emotions.
A. Stress the importance of the correct information processing procedures.
B. Ignore existing procedures to evaluate information.
A. Carefully document the decision-making process.
B. Forget to document the decision-making process.

The choices related to letter A represent the rational thinking while the choices related to letter B represent the intuitive.

- How many As (rational thinking) did you have compared to Bs (intuitive) for this situation?
- In this situation, do you think an opposite approach would have proven more beneficial? Example: if your thinking was rational would an intuitive approach been better to apply?
- If you take this assessment for multiple situations, do you see a trend as to your decision-making process?

Assessment: Predictions Exercise

Directions: assess how sure you are by writing down an answer in each of the following categories. Use some predetermined time period in the near future. For example, "in the next two weeks we will definitely close three new clients." Then, be sure to revisit your answers to see how well you predicted the future.

- It will definitely happen (100% sure).
- It will almost probably happen.
- It is likely to happen.
- It may well happen.
- It might happen.
- It isn't likely to happen.
- It probably won't happen.
- It almost certainly won't happen.
- It definitely won't happen.

CHAPTER 9

Essential Skill 3: Connect and Empower Others

To embrace the ambiguity of a postpandemic world, the third essential skill to develop is to connect and empower others. This has been true throughout history and will continue to be so in the postpandemic period. Making some difference in the lives of others, a theme espoused by authors over the centuries, forms the bedrock of one's purpose and place in society. As individuals found new ways to connect and continue being useful to others, on both a professional and personal level, people around the world leveraged technology such as Zoom, to connect and empower others. According to Zoom, the firm charges businesses for its remote meeting software in addition to more limited free use for the general public, sales skyrocketed 326 percent to $2.6 billion in 2020 while profits jumped from just $21.7 million in 2019 to $671.5 million in 2020.[1] Almost overnight, the virtual connectivity provided a lifeline to people as they looked to stay connected with co-workers, friends, and loved ones. In the postpandemic world, according to Michael R. Nelson, research associate at CSC Leading Edge Forum, observed, "connecting the unconnected is critical if everyone is going to prosper in the post-corona virus disease (COVID)-19 economy."[2]

Those interested in maintaining relevance in the postpandemic world will use their connection to others to empower them to embrace the ambiguity. On the necessity of empowering others, especially employees, Murielle Tiambo, senior engagement manager at PwC in New York noted, "employee empowerment is even more relevant to successfully navigate the coronavirus pandemic."[3] Since organizations had to identify new ways to connect with their employees and clients during the pandemic, "the ability to remain agile and embrace the ambiguity of instituting new ways to stay connected and foster an inclusive team has become an even more essential factor to effective leadership" in the postpandemic market-place.[4] To connect and empower others, history provides evidence of the four strategies included in this section of the training program: practice unbuntu, demonstrate compassion, help others recognize their potential, and offer what others need.

The first strategy to practice the essential skill of connecting and empowering others is to practice unbuntu, derived from a Nguni word, meaning "humanity," or "the quality of being human."[5] Ubuntu has its roots in humanist African philosophy, where the idea of community is one of the building blocks of society. Ubuntu is that nebulous concept of common humanity, oneness: humanity, you, and me both. This African proverb reveals a world view that we owe our selfhood to others, that we are first and foremost social beings, that, if you will, no man/woman is an island, or as the African would have it, "One finger cannot pick up a grain." Ubuntu is, at the same time, a deeply personal philosophy that calls on us to mirror our humanity for each other. Since the transi-tion to democracy in South Africa with the Nelson Mandela presidency in 1994, the term has become more widely known outside of Southern Africa, notably popularized to English-language readers through the ubuntu theology of Desmond Tutu.

In Tutu's book, *No Future Without Forgiveness*, he describes a per-son with ubuntu as "open and available to others, affirming of others … has a proper self-assurance."[6] The ubuntu this person possesses comes from being part of a greater whole. South Africa's postapartheid truth and reconciliation commission, which was chaired by Tutu, would have borrowed from ubuntu philosophy. At Nelson Mandela's memorial in December 2013, U.S. President Barack Obama spoke about Ubuntu, saying: "There is a word in South Africa—Ubuntu—a word that captures Mandela's greatest gift: his recognition that we are all bound together in ways that are invisible to the eye; that there is a oneness to humanity; that we achieve ourselves by sharing ourselves with others, and caring for those around us."[7] This sharing and caring, however, can be difficult at times and involves consideration of the porcupine dilemma.

The porcupine dilemma is a metaphor concerning the dynamics, chal-lenges, and consequences of human intimacy. Both Arthur Schopenhauer and Sigmund Freud have used this situation to describe what they feel is the state of the individual in relation to others in society.[8] According to Schopenhauer, the dilemma exists when porcupines huddle together for warmth on a cold winter day. As they begin to get close to one another, they started to prick one another with their quills. After trying several times to get close to one another, the porcupines learned that the best way to do so would be to remain at some distance from one another. Exploring this balance between the need to be close to one another and the necessity to not prick one another is a social problem. During the pandemic, people around the world lost that ability to even explore physical proximity to others as many governments required people to stay in for long periods of time. During the postpandemic world, people will once again need to develop the essential skill of practicing unbuntu while considering the porcupine dilemma.

Learning how to demonstrate compassion is another strategy to practice the essential skill of connecting and empowering others. People like Pittsburgh Penguin goaltender Matt Murray understand the significance of offering comfort to others, even if they are competitors. During pregame warm-ups on November 27, 2019, Murray skated down the ice to check on Vancouver Canucks goaltender Jacob Markstrom whose father had recently passed away. Murray's father passed away the previous season and offered a heartwarming gesture to Markstrom.[9] Whether it's in the competitive sphere of professional sports, the profit focused business arena, the nonprofit world driven by mission, or a government office motivated by public service, demonstrating compassion continues to grow in significance as an important strategy to consider. For example, in a December 2015 *Harvard Business Review* article, Emma Seppälä and Kim Cameron discussed the impact managers have on the mental health of those they manage and wrote "A brain-imaging study found when employees recalled an unkind or un-empathic boss, they showed increased activation in areas of the brain associated with avoidance and negative emotion while the opposite was true when they recalled an empathic boss."[10] This need to demonstrate compassion accelerated during the pandemic.

In a May 2020 report, the consulting firm McKinsey published findings that identified four qualities available to help leaders find the "compassionate voice to manage in crisis and shepherd their organization into a postcrisis next normal."[11] Attaining a keener sense of self-awareness, exhibiting *vulnerability*, and confronting what is unfolding, demonstrating *empathy* to better tap the emotions of others, and acting with *compassion* to make individuals and groups feel genuinely cared for. Cultivate these qualities in a balanced way by first tuning inward to understand and integrate your own emotions and fears, and then turning outward to alleviate pain, support others, and over time, enable people and the business to recover. A few months after the McKinsey report, Rasmus Hougaard, Jacqueline Carter, and Nick Hobson wrote in the *Harvard Business Review*, "Compassion on its own is not enough." For effective leadership, compassion must be combined with wisdom. By wisdom, we mean leadership competence, a deep understanding of what motivates people and how to manage them to deliver on agreed priorities."[12] To garner this wisdom, Hougaard and colleagues emphasize the need for leaders to increase their self-awareness and self-compassion. "Having genuine compassion for others," they stated, "starts with having compassion for yourself. Self-compassion includes getting quality sleep and taking breaks during the day. For many leaders, self-compassion means letting go of obsessive self-criticism. Stop criticizing yourself for what you could have done differently or better."[13]

A third strategy to practice the essential skill of connecting and empowering others is to help others recognize their potential. In his 2007 book *Don't Make a Black Woman Take Off Her Earrings: Madea's Uninhibited Commentaries on Love and Life*, actor, director, and author Tyler Perry wrote "You will occasionally run into someone who is eager to listen, eager to learn, and willing to try new things. We have a responsibility as parents, older people, teachers, people in the neighborhood to recognize that."[14] Perry recognized that only a few would ever demonstrate this eagerness but when they did, it is critical to recognize, and help develop, their potential. Ashley Lamothe is one such example. In 2011 at the age of 26, Lamothe became Chick-fil-A's youngest Black woman Franchise owner. In 2018, she would open-up her second Chick-fil-A restaurant. Her story has its origins for this native of Marietta, Georgia, when at 15 years of age, she began her relationship with Chick-Fil-A working as a team member. What originally started as a way for Lamothe to make some extra money turned into a significant opportunity for her to create a long-term career path for herself. Once she became a student at nearby Spelman College in Atlanta, she continued to work part-time at Chick-Fil-A and eventually became a director on the leadership team. A pivotal suggestion from one of her supervisors changed the course of her life. Lamothe was pursuing her degree in theater when one day at Chick-Fil-A an operator discussed her long-term ambitions. As Lamothe recalled "during that conversation, the operator recommended that I pursue a career in leadership. I'd never considered it. Sometimes you just need someone to help you see your potential."[15]

Yes, it is indeed true that a Chick-fil-A operator saw potential in Lamothe. It is equally true, however, that Lamothe was, in Perry's words, "eager to listen, eager to learn, and willing to try new things." It is wonderful when someone see potential in you; but are you eager to listen, eager to learn, and willing to try new things? Upon completing Chick-fil-A's leadership program, the executive team asked if she would be willing to move to Los Angeles and open up her first Chick-fil-A restaurant across the street from the University of Southern California. Since she was willing to try new things, Lamothe jumped at the opportunity and in doing so, became the youngest Black franchise owner. To return the favor afforded her years earlier, Lamothe says she is particularly interested in helping others reach their potential and noted "I want to help my team members get to where they want to go, whether it is a career with Chick-fil-A, or studying law or medicine, or anything. I want to help them make that next step."[16] Lamothe's hard work is paying off. In 2018, she was awarded the company's Symbol of Success, an honor reserved for Chick-fil-A Operators whose businesses experience particularly high sales growth.

Offering what others need is another strategy to practice the essential skill of connecting and empowering others. In *How Will You Measure Your Life*, Clayton Christensen shares the story of a fast-food restaurant chain that hired Christensen's research company to understand why 40 percent of milkshakes were purchased in the morning. Interviews with customers who purchased a morning milkshake revealed that they had a long commute to work. The milkshake was easy to drink in the car, filled them until lunch and was enjoyable to drink. The researchers concluded that customers hired the milkshake to do a very specific job. The customers faced a long, boring commute, had one free hand, and needed something to stave off hunger until noon. The milkshake was hired in lieu of a bagel or doughnut because it was relatively tidy and appetite-quenching, and because trying to suck a thick liquid through a thin straw gave customers something to do with their boring commute. To improve customer satisfaction, the "company created a morning milkshake that was even thicker (to last through a long commute) and more interesting (with chunks of fruit) than its predecessor."[17] The chain also created a different milkshake more appealing to parents who wanted to provide a special treat for their children. This milkshake, unlike the morning version, was easier for young children to drink. We can apply the same lessons to our relationships. The milkshake story helps us understand that people in our life need certain things and it is our job to figure out what they need. We can do this by listening, placing aside our own needs, and making ourselves available for those in our life. All too often we think our approach is helpful but what would better serve our relationship is asking the other person "what do you need?" This is especially true in times of crisis such as the COVID-19 global pandemic.

Employees across almost every industry had to quickly pivot to either work at home or learn to perform their job amidst the pandemic. Peoples' needs changed overnight and as a result mental health, already a critical national issue, increased as a pressure point for many. For example, a survey from the Centers for Disease Control and Prevention found that almost 41 percent of American adults struggled with mental health issues stemming from the pandemic.[18] Another study found many adults reporting difficulty sleeping (36%) or eating (32%), increases in alcohol consumption or substance use (12%), and worsening chronic conditions (12%) due to worry and stress over the coronavirus.[19] Anxiety over layoffs, burnout, and mental health were the top three challenges identified by employees. Thus, during the after pandemic period, what employees need is a compassionate management team guided by empathy, understanding, and patience. While the golden rule involves treating others the way you would like them to treat you, perhaps we need to think differently and redefine such an approach in the postpandemic world as "treating others in the way in which they would like to be treated." Doing so would go a long way helping to identify what others need.

The four strategies related to the essential skill of connecting and empowering others are as follows: practice unbuntu, demonstrate compassion, help others recognize their potential, and offer what others need. Janelle Estes emphasized this essential skill in a March 29, 2021 article on the consumer experience as it transitioned from pre-, during, and post-, pandemic. Estes explained how the pandemic caused physical experiences to become primarily digital and people adjusted to a world with limited in-person interaction. As such, it is "increasingly important for companies to meet their customers where they are. Since the pandemic exposed the disconnect between companies and their customers, empathy is essential to making this happen."[20] By acknowledging this gap in empathy, companies have been presented with the unique opportunity in the postpandemic world to embrace the ambiguity and "get closer to the people they are designing experiences for, even if they can't physically be near them."[21] This chapter provided numerous historical examples of how individuals connecting with and empowering others. These lessons are available to anyone willing to engage in the self-reflection, self-awareness, and self-care required to apply such experiences to the postpandemic world. This essential skill of connecting with and empowering others has been around for a long-time and will continue to serve as a viable option for those looking to embrace the ambiguity of the years ahead. Connecting with and empowering others can also help one practice the next essential skill of demonstrating a strong work ethic.

Assessment: Open-Ended Questions

- What are your initial thoughts on unbuntu?
- Do you agree that "one finger cannot pick up a grain?"
- Do you believe "we are all bound together in ways that are invisible to the eye?" Why? Why not?
- Why do you think it is difficult for people to embrace the practice of unbuntu?
- What is the relationship between unbuntu pre- and post-COVID?
- Do you think COVID impacted unbuntu? Explain.
- What are your initial thoughts on the porcupine dilemma?
- How can you reconcile the porcupine dilemma with unbuntu?

- How do you think unbuntu can help you embrace the ambiguity of a postpandemic world?
- Do you have compassion for yourself?
- Are you getting quality sleep?
- Are you taking breaks during the day?
- Are you letting go of self-criticism?
- How often are you increasing your self-awareness?
- How often do you exhibit vulnerability and confront what is unfolding?
- How often are you demonstrating empathy to better tap the emotions of others?
- What obstacles stand in the way and prevent some people from demonstrating compassion?
- Do you think COVID changed how people are compassionate toward themselves or others?
- Has anyone helped you along your journey?
- Have you helped anyone along their journey?
- How does it feel when someone empowers you?
- How do you feel when you empower someone?
- How did the pandemic alter the ways in which people connect with one another?
- How often are you putting in the work to understand those around you?
- How often are you offering what others need?
- How do you know if you are offering what others need?
- If you are a manager or a leader, can you identify multiple times during the pandemic when you offered what others needed?
- During the pandemic, have your bosses offered you what you needed?

Assessment: Self-Care Evaluation

Directions: Using the following scale, rate the following areas in terms of frequency during the last _____ (days or weeks). You decide the period of time involved with this assessment.

5 = Frequently

4 = Occasionally

3 = Rarely

2 = Never

1 = It never occurred to me

Physical Self-Care

____ Eat a healthy diet on a regular schedule (three or more times a day)

____ Include exercise in your daily routine

____ Engage in preventative medical care

____ Use vacation days when necessary

____ Get massages as often as necessary

____ Sleep enough to wake up rested

Psychological Self-Care

____ Set aside time each day for self-reflection

____ Find time to sit in silence

____ Read something unrelated to work

____ Identify a new way to relieve stress

____ Commit to learning something new

Emotional and Spiritual Self-Care

____ Spend time with people who love you

____ Be open to not knowing

____ Take a walk outside, preferably in nature

____ Do something to make yourself laugh

____ Give yourself permission to relax

Workplace or Professional Self-Care

____ Take a break during the workday

____ Take time to chat with co-workers

____ Make quiet time to complete tasks

____ Set limits with your clients and colleagues

____ Arrange your work space so it is comfortable and comforting

Exercise: Empowering Others at Work

Directions: For each of the following 10 tasks available to you for empowering others at work, provide an example of the last time you did so and how often you used this task during the last two weeks.

1. Illustrated how the project or work is directly linked to the organization's vision
2. Define boundaries so everyone involved understands what is expected of them and when
3. Be sure to check your micromanagement hat at the door and focus on finding that balance between direction and support
4. Give people responsibility for the entire project so they feel empowered
5. Create an environment where people can use their skills and maintain a sense of autonomy
6. Encourage the team through regular positive feedback providing a critique, not criticism, when appropriate
7. Allow opportunities for people to learn a new skill they have expressed an interest in acquiring
8. Invite collaboration between individuals or groups that seldom have the opportunity to work together
9. Use the three C approach to communication—be clear, concise, and compelling
10. Celebrate the good work along the way and the success at the end of the project

CHAPTER 10

Essential Skill 4: Demonstrate a Strong Work Ethic

Demonstrating a strong work ethic is the fourth essential skill to develop for those interested in embracing the ambiguity of a postpandemic world. Throughout history, hard work, dedication, and sustained effort over a long period of time have been synonymous with a strong work ethic. In today's postpandemic VUCA world, a strong work ethic needs to combat a society that grows more impatient with each passing day. Thanks to disruptive new technologies that produce instant communication, transactions, and connections, people have grown accustomed to immediate. Whether it is searching the Internet for an answer, texting someone when they are unable to talk, or purchasing an item online, people have grown accustomed to expanding little effort but expecting big results. While much has indeed changed, and will continue to do so, demonstrating a strong work ethic, staying disciplined, and putting in the time are all necessary for those looking to development the habits to achieve and maintain relevance. As professional soccer player Alexandra "Ali" Blaire Krieger tweeted "You can control two things: your work ethic and your attitude about anything."[1] Between her junior and senior year in college, Krieger demonstrated her work ethic and attitude as she had to recover from a pulmonary embolism that affected her blood flow triggering six mini-heart attacks. She was required to do a series of self-injections of enoxaparin for several months, but eventually made a full recovery to play her senior year. To demonstrate a strong work ethic within this context of an essential skill, history provides evidence of the four strategies included in this section of the training program: outwork thousands in front of nobody, improve your daily routine, reflect upon your relationship with desire, and adjust your sails as the winds change.

The first strategy to practice the essential skill of demonstrating a strong work ethic is to outwork thousands in front of nobody. Professional basketball player Damian Lillard believes this is true and wrote "If you want to look good in front of thousands, you have to outwork thousands in front of nobody."[2] After being selected by the Portland Trailblazers with the sixth overall pick in the 2012 NBA draft, Lillard was unanimously voted Rookie of the Year and became one of four players in Trail Blazers franchise history to become a four-time All-Star. Lillard also maintains a high-level of self-awareness and noted "I know what I am as a basketball player and as a person. I do not see myself as above, elevated, or, like, more important than other people. I view myself with people; I don't view myself as a superstar." Lillard wears the jersey number No. 0, representative for the letter "O" and his journey in life; from Oakland (Oakland High School), to Ogden, Utah (Webster State University), and now Oregon (Portland Trail Blazers). Lillard navigated the chaos and practiced the art of living well by understanding the need to "outwork thousands in front of nobody." This mentality of outworking thousands in front of nobody requires relentless practice over an extended period.

According to the research conducted by the University of Nebraska psychologist Richard Dienstbier individuals have the capacity to become mentally and physically stronger with practice. He developed his "toughness model" first published in 1989 in the journal *Psychological Review*. Gathering evidence from a wide range of human and animal studies, he demonstrated that exposure to intermittent stressors, such as cold temperatures and aerobic exercise, made individuals physiologically "tougher."[3] They became less overwhelmed by subsequent difficulties, and by their own fight-or-flight arousal. Interestingly, Dienstbier noted that toughened individuals increasingly seek out experiences that stimulate them and provide opportunities for more mastery and success. One such person who practices getting tougher is Navy SEAL veteran David Goggins. Goggins wrote "It's easy to win when life's your best friend but when it's choking you out is when you truly grow. Sometimes there is no light at the end of the tunnel, but you still must go in! Start conditioning your mind to walk in the darkness. Trust me, the more you walk in it the better your eyes will adjust to it."[4] In his *Embrace the Suck* video, Goggins shares how he overcame a violent father, racism, low self-esteem, and so many debilitating obstacles to later achieve incredible military and personal accomplishments and honors and the mentality that kept him going. As Goggins said, "Growing is a lifestyle. We need friction to grow. I put a bunch of friction in my life, and I grew. You want to get tough; it is a lifestyle."[5] Such a lifestyle, according to Goggins, demanded that one "callous their mind. If you say you are going to wake up at 4:30 in the morning and run, then do it. Do something that sucks every day of your life. That's how you grow."[6] There was no secret to his success. Goggins merely changed his habits and improved his daily routine to alter the course of his life. You have the same option.

Improving upon your daily routine is another strategy to practice the essential skill of demonstrating a strong work ethic. Goggins, like so many others who develop their potential, practice what John C. Maxwell once noted: "You'll never change your life until you change something you do daily. The secret of your success is found in your daily routine."[7] Fellow author Robert Brown Parker had a routine that allowed him to retire from teaching and become a full-time writer. Brown was an American writer of fiction, primarily of the mystery/detective genre. His most famous works were the 40 novels written about the fictional private detective *Spenser*. In an undated interview published on *The Strand Magazine* website, Parker discussed his daily routine and the dynamics involved with it and said "I've always been able to write my quota for the day. I do no fewer than five and no more than ten pages, five days a week, unless there is some event in the family that prohibits that. And frequently after I finish my, let us say 10 pages for the day, I don't know where I'm going. So, the next time I sit down, I find that I do not know what to write. But I just think about it until I do."[8] For this part of the Embracing Ambiguity training program, as is the case with all the other sections, it is important to remind yourself that what works for one person will not necessarily work for another. Your routine should work for you and it should be in alignment with your desire.

A third strategy to practice the essential skill of demonstrating a strong work ethic is reflecting upon your relationship with desire. In the pursuit of such desire, you should consider your relationship with it. The Buddhist collection of thoughts entitled *Mahaprajnaparamita Shastra* noted "When one seeks an object of desire, one suffers. When one gets an object of desire, one fears losing it. When one loses an object of desire, one is greatly troubled. At every point, there is no joy." Have you suffered when seeking an object of desire? Have you feared losing an objective of desire you obtained? Have you been troubled by losing an object you once desired? Your relationship with desire will impact your ability to navigate the chaos and practice the art of living well.

Part of your relationship with desire should involve an understanding that, as British Nobel laureate Bertrand Arthur William Russell observed "All human activity is prompted by desire. There is a wholly fallacious theory advanced by some earnest moralists to the effect that it is possible to resist desire in the interests of duty and moral principle. I say this is fallacious." On the observations that "all human activity is prompted by desire" Dr. Galen Guengerich wrote in an October 16, 2015, *Psychology Today* article "The Four States of Desire: From Everything to One Thing" there are several desires humans experience. "Physical desire is called hunger or thirst; intellectual desire is called curiosity; sexual desire is called lust; economic desire is called consumer demand. Remove these expressions of desire, and human life as we know it would cease to exist."[9] For many people, they view life as a desire for wanting things and experiences they do not have. The 15th-century Indian mystic Kabir identified four states of desire: countless, limited, few, and one. Most people are born with countless desires that concern the superficial aspects of life such as personal appearance or personal possessions. Individuals with limited desires lead what many would consider successful lives but manage to accomplish modest goals, because they can focus on only some desires. Great musicians, poets, and scientists such as Madame Curie and Albert Einstein, have few desires, and make their mark in their respective fields. The fourth category is the rarest of groups and only have one desire. These are the great mystics—spiritual leaders who often practice meditation, which is a demanding discipline designed to reduce one's number of desires. As one considers reducing the number of desires as they age to improve their work ethic, so too can then adjust their sails to move forward amidst the ambiguity of a postpandemic society.

Adjusting your sails to propel forward is another strategy to practice the essential skill of demonstrating a strong work ethic. Avoiding storms is virtually impossible. People who grow both personally and professionally understand this and leverage the wind from a storm to propel them forward. In 1859, the well-known spiritualist Cora L. V. Hatch delivered a lecture at the Cooper Institute and said, "You could not prevent a thunderstorm, but you could use the electricity; you could not direct the wind, but you could trim your sail so as to propel your vessel as you pleased, no matter which way the wind blew."[10] Adjusting sails is akin to leaving your comfort zone and engaging in the work ethic, the situation demands of you. Actor Jean Smart demonstrated a strong work ethic when she adjusted her sails after her husband of 34 years, Richard Gilliland, passed away in March 2020, with a week's left of filming to do for her HBO series *Hacks*. What propelled Smart outside of her comfort zone and kept her going during such a tragic time? As she told, *NPR* "When Richard passed, I had to finish the show. It was very scary and distressing, but I had to. As the lead on the show, I felt a huge responsibility to the crew and the cast."[11] Fellow actor Vincent D'Ornofio used a similar strategy and in so doing altered the course of his life and career.

While working as a bouncer at the Hard Rock Café and acting in New York theater, fellow actor Matthew Modine and his wife bumped into D'Ornofio one night at the restaurant. According to D'Ornofio, "Matthew said he was doing this Stanley Kubrick thing and there was a part available. I did not even think about being in film. I saw a lot of films, but I thought of film actors as very different from myself."[12] Encouraged by his friend, D'Ornofio sent audition tapes to Kubrick in England. Much to his surprise, Kubrick cast D'Ornofio as Pvt. Leonard Lawrence, an overweight, clumsy Marine recruit in the movie *Full Metal Jacket*. This role would be the defining moment in his acting career. Originally, the character of Pvt. Lawrence had been written as a "skinny ignorant redneck"; however, Kubrick believed the role would have more impact if the character were big and clumsy. D'Onofrio gained 70lbs for the role and had his weight balloon from 210lbs to 280lbs.[13] This remains the record for most weight gained by an actor for a film. Reflecting back upon his career D'Onofrio said "Stanley made my career. There is no question about that. I have done over 50 films because of him. Because of that part. There is no other reason why I am working as an actor."[14] D'Onofrio adjusted his sails and considered the role, sent Kubrick audition tapes, gained 70lbs, and in so doing completely altered his life and career.

To demonstrate a strong work ethic, this section of the training program examined the four strategies of: outworking thousands in front of nobody, improving your daily routine, reflecting upon your relationship with desire, and adjusting your sails as the winds change. Reflecting upon his work ethic and daily routine Scott Adams, cartoonist, and entrepreneur, suggested that the most important trick for maximizing productivity is matching one's mental state to the task. For example, Adams understood his early morning hours were the most productive. According to Adamas, "When I first wake up, my brain is relaxed and creative. The thought of writing a comic is fun, and it's relatively easy because my brain is in exactly the right mode for that task."[15] If he tried being creative in the afternoon, it would be "a waste of time." As the postpandemic world provides new opportunities to demonstrate a strong work ethic, it is important to remember that sometimes life should be lived as an experiment in order to explore and discover. This chapter provided numerous examples of how individuals demonstrated a strong work ethic. These lessons are available to anyone willing to engage in the self-reflection, self-awareness, and self-care required to apply such experiences to the postpandemic world.

This essential skill of demonstrating a strong work ethic has been around for a long-time and will continue to serve as a viable option for those looking to embrace the ambiguity of the years ahead. In the first season, second episode of the HBO series *Hacks*, Deborah Vance (portrayed by Jean Smart) as a legendary Las Vegas comedian, is stuck in the desert with her 25-year-old writer and assistant Ava (portrayed by Hannah Einbinder). After Ava cries about life being so hard, Deborah turns to her and raises her voice telling her young colleague "Good is the minimum. It's the baseline. You have to be so much more than good. And even if you're great and lucky, you still have to work really f&%^* hard."[16] But the character of Deborah Vance, like so many others in real like who possess a strong work ethic understand, "even that is not enough. You have to scratch and claw and it never f&%^* ends." Demonstrating a strong work ethic can also help one practice the next essential skill of experimenting with life."[17]

Assessment: The Iceberg Illusion

Directions: A good exercise for this Essential Skill is to think of an iceberg. Most people only think about, see, and consider the tip of the iceberg. Failing to notice the underneath of an iceberg, can have significant consequences. For today's reflection, success is the tip of the iceberg. What you fail to see are the thousands of hours someone put in as well as the disappointments, frustrations, late nights, rejections, struggles, discipline, criticism, failures, doubts, stress, and risks involved. How often do you outwork thousands in front of nobody? If you are willing to do so, how long would you be able to keep up that level of practice? A week? A month? A year? Several years? How often do you do something that sucks to grow? Have you looked at someone success and wondered how many disappointments, rejections, or failures were involved?

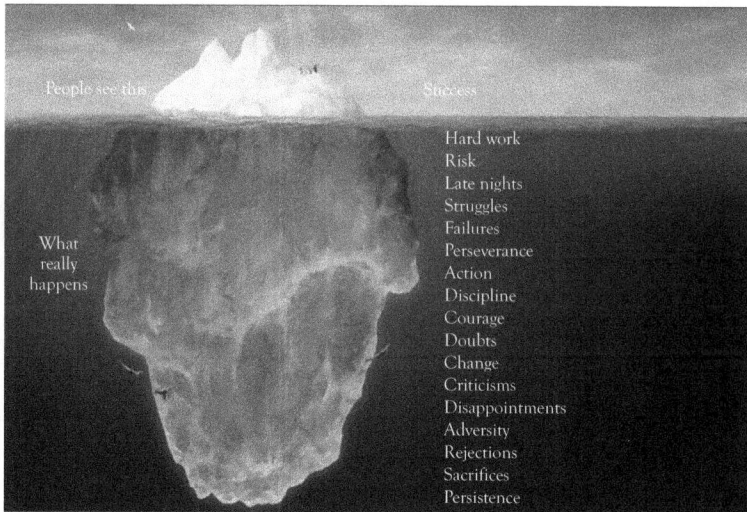

Directions: Using the following blank iceberg image, fill in the following two sections:

- The top of the iceberg above the water—this is what others see of you. Example: Vice-President, Director, or Manager.
- The bottom of the iceberg below the surface—write down what it took for you to get to where you are but so few people recognize about you.

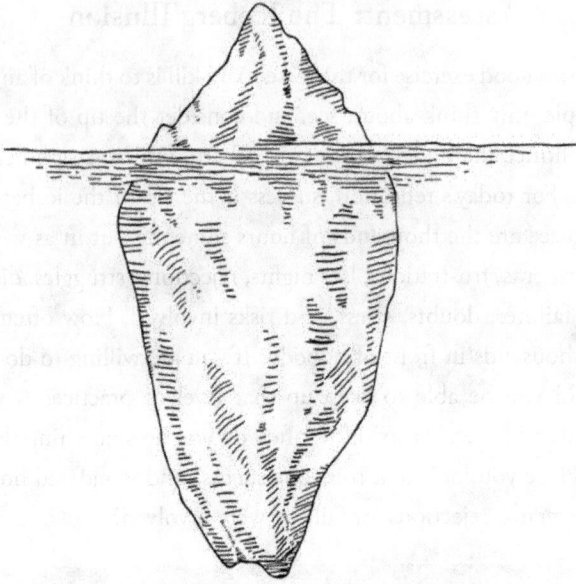

Assessment: Open-Ended Questions

- Do you have the mentality to outwork thousands in front of nobody?
- Can you engage in relentless practice over an extended period?
- Do you have role models of others who engage in relentless practice to refer to?
- How many desires do you have: countless, limited, few, or one?
- How do you know?
- How often do you think about your desires?
- Have your desires changed over time?
- How often do you set time aside to understand your relationship with desire?
- What internal or external factors contribute to your desires changing?
- What is it that you want?
- How often do you reflect upon your daily routine?
- When is the last time you altered your daily routine?
- How did you change your routine?

- How long did it take you to see a positive result of the change in your daily routine?
- How often do you adjust your sails?
- How comfortable are you changing direction?
- Why do you think you are comfortable/uncomfortable adjusting your sails?
- Are you afraid of going in a new life direction? Why/Why not?

Exercise: The Link Between Habits and Priorities

Directions: There's an adage that is often referred to as "you are what you repeatedly do." What do you repeatedly do? What are your daily habits? And what is the link between your habits and your priorities? This exercise challenges you to reflect upon how you use each day and what or who you make a priority. Using the following picture of the four elements of rocks, pebbles, sand, and water, describe how you would fill the empty jar.

To guide your decision-making process, here are the definitions of each item:

- Rocks: represent the highest priorities with the greatest value.
- Pebbles: represent a high priority but not nearly as important or valuable as the rocks.
- Sand: small tasks that have their place but fall a distant third to the rocks and pebbles.
- Water: trivial time wasters.

Part I: identify your rocks, pebbles, sand, and water.

- Rocks:
- Pebbles:
- Sand:
- Water:

Part II: explain what you would place in the jar first, then second, and so on.

CHAPTER 11

Essential Skill 5: Experiment With Your Life

To embrace the ambiguity of a postpandemic world, the fifth essential skill to develop is to experiment with your life. A young woman once asked French Cuban American Anaïs Nin, how does one go about figuring out what to do with their life? The young woman was struggling with this question. In her response, Nin emphasized the need to experiment with one's life, embrace the mistakes made along the way as they provide invaluable lessons, and be open to an unfolding of your life. Nin referred the young woman to Gauguin who decided at a certain point he was not a banker anymore as he wished to be a painter. Gauguin experimented with this life and walked away from banking. Having the ability to alter one's direction in life, Nin argued, was a necessary skill to practice since "society keeps demanding that we fit in and not disturb things. They would like you to fit in right away so that things work now."[1] Experimenting with one's life was a far better approach to living. Evidence of such experimentation can be found throughout business literature. For example, in his *Harvard Business Review* blog post, Peter Bregman added the observation that "Most successful people and businesses have meandered their way to success by being willing to exercise their talents in ways they never would have imagined at the onset."[2] Thus, experimenting with life is commonplace for individuals and organizations alike. Remember, experimenting with one's life can include small tasks. Dr. Alice Boyes, for example, prefers shorter self-experiments as they have the advantage of being particularly nonthreatening and give individuals the opportunity to try a wider variety of new behaviors.[3] To experiment with your life, history provides evidence of the four strategies included in this section of the training program: move forward without a plan, get into the arena of life, go out and meet glory and danger alike, and be afraid but do it anyway.

The first strategy to practice the essential skill of experimenting with your life is to move forward without a plan. MacArthur Fellow and anthropologist Jason De Léon said, "Most of my career has been defined by making it up as I go along."[4] Two examples of others who moved forward without a plan are Chobani founder Hamdi Ulukaya and actor Dennis Farina. In a *60 Minutes* interview Ulukaya said "The poet Rumi wrote 'As you start to walk on the way, the way appears.' When I started Chobani, I'd never run a company before and there was no plan."[5] Ulukaya is a Turkish businessman, entrepreneur, investor, and philanthropist based in the United States. Ulukaya is the owner, founder, Chairman, and CEO of Chobani, the #1-selling strained yogurt (Greek-style) brand in the United States. Originating from a dairy-farming family in a small village in Turkey, Ulukaya immigrated to the United States in 1994 to study English and took a few business courses as well. In an interview with *CNN Money*, Ulukaya explains that he was serious about Kurdish rights and left Turkey due to the Turkish state's oppression of its Kurdish minority group. He started a modest feta-cheese factory in 2002 on the advice of his father. His larger success came from taking a major risk: Ulukaya purchased a large, defunct yogurt factory in upstate New York in 2005, in a region that used to be the center of a dairy and cheese industry. With no prior experience in the yogurt business, he has created a yogurt empire, Chobani, with facilities in several states.[6] It was valued at over $1 billion in annual sales in less than five years after launch, becoming the leading yogurt brand in the United States by 2011. Ulukaya figured out a way to translate his dream into reality without a plan or a path. So too did actor Dennis Farina.

Reflecting upon his career path Farina said, "I never had a grand plan with what I was going to do."[7] Before becoming an actor, Farina served three years in the U.S. Army and then 18 years in the Chicago Police Department's burglary division, from 1967 to 1985. He had been working as a detective when a mutual friend introduced him to the director Michael Mann, who was making his first feature film in 1981, *Thief*. Mr. Farina was initially a consultant for the movie before being given a small role as a crime boss's enforcer. For several years afterward, Mr. Farina juggled his police job with local theater roles and appearances in movies and television shows. He was often cast by Mr. Mann, including in several episodes of his hit show *Miami Vice*. Farina quit police work after Mr. Mann cast him in 1986 in the NBC series "Crime Story." He would go on to spend four decades in film and television with a two-season stint in *Law & Order* as Detective Joe Fontana.

Getting into the arena of life is another strategy to practice the essential skill of experimenting with your life. On April 23, 1910, Theodore Roosevelt gave what would become one of the most widely quoted speeches of his career. After leaving office the previous year to spend a year hunting in Central Africa and then touring Northern Africa and Europe, the former President attended events and gave speeches throughout 1910 in places such as Cairo, Berlin, Naples, and Oxford. He stopped at the Sorbonne in Paris on April 23 and delivered a speech called "Citizenship in a Republic," which, among some, would come to be known as "The Man in the Arena." His speech included references to his family history, war, human and property rights, the responsibilities of citizenship, and France's falling birthrate. But Roosevelt also used this opportunity to proclaim two inspirational and impassioned messages. In his first proclamation, he railed against cynics who looked down at men who were trying to make the world a better place when he said: "The poorest way to face life is to face it with a sneer."[8] It is a weak person who practices a cynical habit of thought and speech, who readily criticizes work which the critic himself never tries to perform, and who maintains an intellectual aloofness which will not accept contact with life's realities.

Roosevelt's second proclamation, however, would continue to echo to the present day over a century later. In the following passage, he refers to the man in the arena and said: "It is not the critic who counts; not the man who points out how the strong man stumbles, or where the doer of deeds could have done them better. The credit belongs to the man who is actually in the arena."[9] For Roosevelt, the man in the arena has a face "marred by dust and sweat and blood; who strives valiantly; who errs, who comes short again and again, because there is no effort without error and shortcoming; but who does actually strive to do the deeds." The one in life's arena "knows great enthusiasms, the great devotions; who spends himself in a worthy cause; who at the best knows in the end the triumph of high achievement, and who at the worst, if he fails, at least fails while daring greatly, so that his place shall never be with those cold and timid souls who neither know victory nor defeat."[10] As a person in the arena, one would often go out to meet glory and danger alike.

A third strategy to practice the essential skill of experimenting with your life is to go out to meet glory and danger alike. People who embrace the ambiguity often have a clear vision of what is before them, glory, and danger alike, yet move forward amidst the ambiguity. In *The Peloponnesian War*, Athenian historian and general Thucydides recalled the words from the politician Pericles who gave a Funeral Oration at the annual observation of the war dead and said, "the bravest are surely those who have the clearest vision of what is before them, glory and danger alike, and yet notwithstanding, go out to meet it."[11] It is easy to walk forward when you know there is glory ahead of you. But how often do you move forward knowing that danger may also cross your path? One such person who went out to meet glory and danger alike was William Pitsenbarger, also known as Pits, grew up in Piqua, Ohio, and dreamed of quitting high school to join the Green Berets. However, he remained in school. After graduating in 1962, Pitsenbarger joined the Air Force. Pitsenbarger began his service in a series of rigorous military schools. These schools included U.S. Army parachute school, survival school, rescue and survival medical course, and the U.S. Navy's scuba diving school. Three years after joining the Air Force, Pitsenbarger arrived in Vietnam in August 1965. Here, he would complete missions as part of Detachment Six of the U.S. Air Force's 38th Aerospace Rescue and Recovery Squadron. On Pitsenbarger's path serving as a pararescueman, he completed more than 250 missions.

During one of his missions in Saigon, Pitsenbarger hung from an HH-43's cable to rescue a wounded South Vietnamese soldier from a burning minefield. His actions earned him an Airman's Medal and the Republic of Vietnam's Medal of Military Merit and Gallantry Cross with bronze palm. Pitsenbarger was killed in action April 11, 1966.[12] A battalion of Viet Cong surrounded 134 soldiers from the First Infantry Division in the thick jungle near Saigon. Due to the rapidly increasing casualties and injuries, the only way to evacuate the wounded from the dense battle zone was with the U.S. Air Force HH-43 Huskie helicopters. Pitsenbarger volunteered to be lowered to the ground to help despite being under fire. Integral to the mission, Pitsenbarger rescued nine soldiers on several trips. When it came time to return to the helicopter, he chose to remain and help the troops. While on the ground, he helped deliver ammunition and give aid to the surviving soldiers under fire. During the battle, he was mortally wounded. He was 21 years old.[13]

Being afraid of something yet doing it anyway is another strategy to practice the essential skill of experimenting with your life. People such as actor Carrie Fisher believe "Stay afraid but do it anyway. What is important is the action. You do not have to wait to be confident. Just do it and eventually the confidence will follow."[14] Fisher was born on October 21, 1956, the daughter of Academy Award-nominated actress Debbie Reynolds and pop singer Eddie Fisher. With her parent's divorce, Fisher turned to books and acting. She never finished high school because she appeared in the musical *Irene* alongside her mother. Fisher made her film debut in *Shampoo* (1975) but it was *Star Wars* that catapulted her to international fame. In a 2011 interview, she said that when she got cast in a "little science fiction film," she just thought of it as a bit of fun. But the film "exploded across the firmament of pop culture, taking all of us along with it; it tricked me into becoming a star all on my own." Over the following decades Fisher appeared in other *Star Wars* films, stared in other movies, and wrote several books. Unfortunately, Fisher experienced trouble with alcohol and drugs. In 1985, for example, she was rushed to a hospital after accidentally taking an overdose of sleeping pills and prescription drugs. Fisher also openly discussed her battle with bipolar disorder. Carrie Fisher's fame as an actress may have rested on just one role in *Star Wars* but she portrayed a character that would become one of the best known in film history. She was remarkably frank about her personal difficulties she fought to overcome. "There's a part of me that gets surprised when people think I am brave to talk about what I've gone through she once said, 'I was brave to last through it.'"[15]

English actress Dame Helen Lydia Mirren said "Don't be afraid of fear, Throw caution to the winds. Look fear straightaway in its ugly face and barge forward. And when you get past it, turn around and give it a good, swift kick in the ass."[16] American writer and comedian Elna Baker wrote "Impossible is just a big word thrown around by small men who find it easier to live in the world they've been given than to explore the power they have to change it. Impossible is not a fact. It's an opinion. Impossible is not a declaration. It's a dare. Impossible is potential. Impossible is temporary."

In a 2017 interview with Amelia Diamond published in "It's Never Too Late: 3 Women on Second Chances and Changing Careers," Polly Rodriguez, Chief Executive Officer and founder of Unbound, said "Be relentless and fearless about learning as much as you can. To be successful you have to enjoy constantly being in over your head every single day."[17]

On confronting fear to move forward, author Carl Richards discussed his preference of being in over his head because it forces him to "perform in ways the shallow end never does. I go from thinking I am capable of 'X' to very quickly performing twice or three times that amount—and sometimes even 10x."[18] Like Richards, American actress Gilda Radner practiced the strategy of experimenting with her life and wrote "Some stories do not have a clear beginning, middle, and end. Life is about not knowing, having to change, taking the moment, and making the best of it, without knowing what is going to happen next. Delicious Ambiguity."[19] Embracing the ambiguity of the postpandemic world requires you to experiment with your life. Such a strategy will challenge you to move forward without a plan, get into the arena of life, go out and meet glory and danger alike, and be afraid but do it anyway. This chapter provided numerous examples of how individuals were able experiment with life. Such experimentation took place prior to the pandemic and should continue as societies emerge in the postpandemic VUCA world. These lessons are available to anyone willing to engage in the self-reflection, self-awareness, and self-care required to apply such experiences to the postpandemic world. This essential skill of experimenting with life has been around for a long-time and will continue to serve as a viable option for those looking to embrace the ambiguity of the years ahead. Experimenting with life can also help one practice the next essential skill of getting comfortable in uncomfortable situations.

Assessment: Open-Ended Questions

- How often can you move forward without a plan?
- Do you face life with a sneer?
- How often do you find yourself a cynic?
- How often does your sneering and cynicism prevent you from navigating the chaos and practicing the art of living well?

- How often do you criticize those attempting something you yourself will not try?
- How often do you point out how the strong man stumbles?
- How often is your face marred with dust and sweat and blood from the daily grind of translating one dream after another into reality?
- How often do you spend yourself in a worthy cause?
- How often do you fail while daring greatly?
- How often are you in the arena?
- If you are not in the arena of life as much as you would like, what, or who, is holding you back? Why are you letting yourself be held back?
- What action step would you need to take to get into the arena of life?
- How often do you venture out to meet glory and danger alike?
- What is your current relationship with impossible?
- How often do you even think about your relationship with impossible?
- Have you often wondered how someone accomplished something you thought impossible?
- How often do you get in over your head?

Assessment: Your Plan Type

Directions: Identify which of the following categories you fall into most of the time. To assess your answer, ask other people to complete this with you in mind. For example, you might ask your co-worker of two years what she thinks your plan type is; she might say 3 but you have selected 6 for yourself. If there is such a disconnect, explore why that is.

1. You need to have a guarantee that your plan will get you to the destination.
2. You need to see the entire plan from beginning to end prior to starting.
3. You need to see most of the plan from beginning to end prior to starting.

4. You need to know the plan has a beginning, middle, and end and can start as information is provided to you along the way.

5. You need to know the destination and have an idea of a path to follow to get there.

6. You can move forward with a plan but are comfortable changing it to get to the predetermined destination.

7. You can move forward without a plan but having a destination in mind.

8. You can move forward without a plan or a destination.

Exercise: Experiment With Your Behavior and Life

Directions: Complete the following behavioral exercise for an upcoming event and reflect upon the results of your experiment.

- Situation: having dinner with my in-laws.
- Prediction: I will need to drink before, during, and after dinner to get through the evening.
- Experiment: Instead of my usual six drinks for such an evening, limit myself to one drink during dinner by focusing on my partner, my breathing, and finding joy in the moment.
- Outcome: Went to dinner without drinking and was a bit more nervous than usual. Focus my attention on my partner and remained aware of my breathing the entire evening. Doing so distracted my attention and at the end of the night realized I had never finished even my one drink.
- What was learned: I managed to successfully experiment with my life to change my behavior ever so slightly. This increased level of self-awareness provided me with a basis for which to conduct future experiments.

- Situation:
- Prediction:
- Outcome:
- What was learned:

CHAPTER 12

Essential Skill 6: Get Comfortable in Uncomfortable Situations

Getting comfortable in uncomfortable situations is the sixth essential skill to develop for those interested in embracing the ambiguity of a post-pandemic world. The COVID-19–related restrictions imposed upon individuals around the world created a variety of uncomfortable living situations. Some individuals were left alone. Roommate or partners living together had to figure out a way to work in close quarters. Parents needed to learn how to work and help their children throughout the school day. The perceived "normalcy" of the prepandemic world convinced people life was certain. But life has never been certain. If people want to live life fully, they need to understand the necessity of being able to live life fully in times of uncertainty. This pandemic served as a tremendous wake-up call to life's uncertainty. Recognizing the uncertainty of life allows people to fully embrace their present circumstances. Managing through the uncomfortableness, and reflecting upon lessons learned during the process, empowers one to gain the self-awareness required to embrace ambiguity. As Chris Parrott noted, "Instead of fighting against the feeling that we are uncomfortable, we can use it for what it is—an indication that a challenge needs our attention and problem-solving skills."[1] To help people improve their problem-solving skills and get comfortable in uncomfortable situations, history provides evidence of the four strategies included in this section of the training program: travel outside of life's comfort zone, outgrow your shoes, learn to manage fear, and navigate the intersection of fear and grit.

The first strategy to practice the essential skill of getting comfortable in uncomfortable situations is to travel outside of life's comfort zone.

People only grow when they are uncomfortable. Many observers believe the adage "life begins at the end of your comfort zone." Stepping outside one's comfort zone is an important, and almost universal, factor in personal growth. Reaching new heights involves the risk of attempting something others thought impossible. Throughout the course of human history, individuals who have accomplished extraordinary feats almost always traveled outside of their comfort zone. The phrase "if it was easy everyone would do it," comes to mind here. Embracing ambiguity is not supposed to be easy. That is why this publication provides a training program for those willing to put in the time to learn, apply, and reflect upon the process. One such example from history of a person who traveled outside of his comfort zone was Roger Bannister. Prior to 1954, many people believed that running a mile under 4 minutes was impossible. The prevailing thought was that the human body was incapable of tolerating the level of uncomfortableness associated with running a sub-4-minute mile. No one had traveled that far out of their comfort zone to achieve such a remarkable physical accomplishment. That all changed on May 6, 1954, when Bannister convinced himself he could break the sub-4-minute mile barrier. On that day, not succumbing to the idea that it was impossible, he ran the mile in 3 minutes and 59.4 seconds. Upon reflection as to how he stepped outside of his comfort zone to set a new world record, Bannister said, "The man who can drive himself further once the effort gets painful is the man who will win."[2] Driving yourself further once the pain kicks in, that is what it takes to travel far outside of your comfort zone. For Bannister, he traveled outside of his comfort zone, pushed himself through the pain, and in so doing, showed others the impossible was indeed possible. But history teaches us another lesson if we look at the fascinating developments regarding the mile race in the aftermath of Bannister's world record. As he noted, "There was a mystique, a belief that it couldn't be done, but I think it was more of a psychological barrier than a physical barrier."[3]

Fifty-six days after Bannister showed the world, a sub-4-minute mile was indeed possible, fellow runner John Landy ran the 4-minute mile in 3 minutes and 57.9 seconds in Finland. Bannister and Landy would race each other in the Mile of the Century where Bannister won in 3 minutes and 58.8 seconds. Within three years, by the end of 1957, 16 other runners also cracked the 4-minute mile.[4] Think about that for a moment. What was once thought impossible, was now done by 16 other runners. Bannister showed the world what was possible; a new normal if you will. Once Bannister did what almost everyone thought impossible, it suddenly became possible. Running a sub-4 would eventually become the standard by which mile runners were measured. The breaking of the 4-minute mile was so significant that *Forbes* names it as one of the greatest athletic achievements of all time.[5] Eventually, the sub-4 became so common place a new measure took its place in the time of a sub-3:50. Hicham El Guerrouj (Morocco) is the current men's record holder with his time of 3:43.13, while Svetlana Masterkova (Russia) has the women's record of 4:12.56. Bannister's sub-4 proved inspirational for runners of all ages as Jim Ryun became the first high school athlete to run a sub-4-minute mile in 1965. According to a *Track & Field News* list, 487 Americans had run a sub-4-minute mile as of June 3, 2017, and 2016 was the year with the newest additions to the list (27), followed by 2015 (24), 2013 (23), and 2012 (also 23).[6] In the postpandemic world, traveling outside of your comfort zone can serve as a useful strategy as you practice getting comfortable in uncomfortable situations.

Outgrowing your shoes is another strategy to practice the essential skill of getting comfortable in uncomfortable situations. History is littered with individuals who challenged themselves to successfully transition from who they are to who they wanted to be. People who "outgrow their shoes" maintain the self-awareness, self-discipline, and self-care required to do what needs to be done in order for them to get comfortable in uncomfortable situations. Alexi Pappas is one such individual. When she was four years old, her mother died by suicide, drastically altering the course of Pappas' life, and setting her on a search for female role models and learning to deal with the loss of her mother at such a young age. Eventually, Pappas turned to running, which provided her with an outlet where she discovered her ability to compete at the highest levels. Over the years, Pappas, the Olympic athlete, would also become known as a filmmaker and award-winning writer. Pappas has succeeded in all three fields because of her ability to commit to personal growth and development. As a runner, she was a National Collegiate Athletic Association (NCAA)

All-American at the indoor 3,000 meters race, 5,000 meters, and the steeplechase as well as the Ivy League champion in the steeplechase. In the
2016 Summer Olympics Women's 10-kilometer race, Pappas represented
Greece and set a national Greek record.

As a filmmaker, Pappas directed, cowrote, and starred in *Tracktown*,
a 2016 American drama and coming of age sports film and also co-wrote
and starred alongside Nick Kroll in *Olympic Dreams*, the first nondocu-
mentary-style movie to ever be filmed at the Olympic Games. As a writer,
Pappas has had her writing appear in a number of publications and her
autobiography *Brave: Chasing Dreams, Befriending Pain, and Other Big
Ideas* was released in January 2021.[7] In the book, she fearlessly and hon-
estly shares her battle with post-Olympic depression and describes how
she emerged on the other side as a thriving and self-actualized woman.
To succeed as a runner, writer, and film maker, Alexi Pappas exemplifies someone who gets comfortable in uncomfortable situations by outgrowing her shoes and continually challenging herself to grow. As Pappas
said: "I think the best choice that I've made is to never plan more than a
year in advance for my life. I have embraced my own growth every year
and allowed myself to outgrow my shoes."[8] The *New York Times* labeled
Pappas a "Renaissance runner"[9] due to her success on multiple fronts.
By practicing the strategy of outgrowing her shoes, Pappas provides an
excellent example of someone who had to learn how embrace the ambiguity of life after her mother's suicide. Through self-care, patience, and
dedication, Pappas repeatedly showcased the value of getting comfortable
in uncomfortable situations.

A third strategy to practice the essential skill of getting comfortable
in uncomfortable situations is to learn how to manage fear. The 2001
novel *Life of Pi*, by Canadian author Yann Martel, tells the story of protagonist Piscine Molitor "Pi" Patel, an Indian Tamil boy from Pondi-
cherry, India. Initially rejected by five London publishing houses, the
novel was accepted by Knopf Canada, published in September 2001,
and has since sold more than 10 million copies worldwide. In the novel,
Pi explores a variety of issues related to spirituality and metaphysics
throughout his life. He survives 227 days after a shipwreck while
stranded on a lifeboat in the Pacific Ocean with a Bengal tiger which
raises questions about the nature of reality and how it is perceived and

told. Fear is one of the emotions explored in the novel and Martel made several observations on how to manage "life's only true opponent." Martel believed that "Only fear can defeat life. It is a clever, treacherous adversary and shows no mercy. It goes for your weakest spot. It begins in your mind."[10] To manage this greatest of adversaries, Martel wrote one "shine the light of words upon it. Because if you don't, if your fear becomes a wordless darkness that you avoid you open yourself to further attacks of fear because you never truly fought the opponent who defeated you."[11] This concept of managing fear to get comfortable in uncomfortable situations has been practiced by many throughout history.

In addition to Martel, best-selling author Judy Blume confronted the fear involved with writing young adult novels about topics some consider taboo such as masturbation, menstruation, birth control, and death. She has had to deal with criticism from individuals and groups that would like to see her books banned. The American Library Association (ALA) has named Blume as one of the most frequently challenged authors of the 21st century. Despite her critics, Blume's books have sold over 82 million copies and they have been translated into 32 languages.[12] On a personal level, Blume has also confronted fear. On August 15, 1959, in the summer of her freshman year of college, she married John M. Blume, who she had met while a student at New York University. He became a lawyer, while she was a homemaker before supporting her family by teaching and writing. They had two children, but the couple divorced in 1976 with Blume later describing the marriage as "suffocating." Shortly after her separation, she met Thomas A. Kitchens, a physicist. The couple married and moved to New Mexico for Kitchens' work. They divorced in 1978. She later spoke about their split: "It was a disaster, a total disaster. After a couple years, I got out. I cried every day. Anyone who thinks my life is cupcakes is all wrong."[13] As Blume wrote "Each of us must confront our own fears, must come face to face with them. How we handle our fears will determine where we go in our lives. To experience adventure or to be limited by the fear of it."[14] A third person who exemplified what it means to manage fear and, as Blume described it, "experience adventure" as a result of doing so is director Steven Spielberg.

The 1975 American thriller film *Jaws* directed by Steven Spielberg and based on Peter Benchley's 1974 novel offers just one example of how Spielberg used fear to push him. Despite the movie's tremendous success, *Jaws* had to overcome a variety of obstacles that included:

1. The original stuntman the studio hired was not suited for the job;
2. The young director demanded perfection and refused to shoot in a tank;
3. The movie's budget more than doubled and went from $3.5 million to $8 million;
4. The shooting schedule tripled from an original 55 to 159 days;
5. The mechanical sharks began to deteriorate in salt water; and
6. The ships started to sink.

Jaws producer David Brown said, "There were times early in the picture when we felt we had made a mistake hiring Steven who was maddeningly perfectionistic … and I have to hand it to him for sticking to his guns."[15] In a *New York Times* interview, Spielberg explained his method that allowed him to stick to his guns when he said: "Every movie I make, there's a hurdle to it. I look for things that will scare me. Fear is my fuel. I get to the brink of not really knowing what to do and that's when I get my best ideas."[16] For those willing to venture outside and get comfortable in uncomfortable situation, Spielberg reminded people while *Jaws* became wildly successful, he still looks back on the filming of that movie as "my most unhappy time in my life as a filmmaker because whole days would go by and we wouldn't get a shot."[17] Embracing ambiguity by getting comfortable in uncomfortable situations has been around for decades, even if it means being unhappy for a while as you work through the situation.

Navigating the intersection of fear and grit is another strategy to practice the essential skill of getting comfortable in uncomfortable situations. Johann Wolfgang von Goethe wrote "The heights charm us, but the steps do not; with the mountain in our view, we love to walk the plains."[18] One such person who understands this connection between fear and grit is Alex Honnold. Honnold is an American rock climber best known for his free-solo ascents of big walls and once thought impossible climbing routes. Free solo is where an individual climbs alone without ropes, harnesses, or other protective equipment, forcing them to rely entirely on their own individual preparation, strength, and skill. Free soloing is the most dangerous form of climbing. On June 3, 2017, he made the first free-solo ascent of El Capitan, completing the 2,900-foot Freerider route in 3 hours and 56 minutes.[19] The feat, described by many as "one of the great athletic feats of any kind, ever," was documented by climber and photographer Jimmy Chin, and was the subject of the 2018 documentary *Free Solo*. To understand his remarkable physical achievement, it is necessary to reflect upon three specific connections between fear and grit: practice, study, and execution.

The first connection between fear and grit involves years of practice. Honnold started climbing at the age of five and spent 10 years inside learning the fundamentals until they became routine. After 10 years of being inside, he ventured outside and took on more challenging climbs with each passing year. As Honnold stated, "After a decade of climbing mostly indoors, I made the transition to the outdoors and gradually started free soloing. I built up my comfort over time and slowly took on bigger and more challenging walls."[20] The second connection between fear and grit involves deep self-awareness. Honnold took the time to study other climbers and then measured himself against them to increase his self-awareness. According to Honnold "I've never been gifted. There were a lot of other kids stronger than me. I just loved climbing, and I've been climbing ever since, so I've naturally gotten better at it."[21] The third connection between fear and grit involves combining the years of practice with a deep sense of self-awareness, so the impossible task of free soloing becomes possible. Upon reflection, Honnold noted that climbing without fear is impossible. He memorized his free solo route, so there was no possibility of error. As he said "I did not want to be wondering if I was going the right way or using the best holds. I needed everything to feel automatic. Once I was on the climb, it was just a matter of executing."[22] Like others before him who got comfortable in uncomfortable situations by navigating the intersection of fear and grit, Honnold embraced the ambiguity of free soloing and in so doing became an inspiration for so many.

To embrace the ambiguity of the postpandemic VUCA world, it will be imperative to learn how to manage fear and get comfortable in uncomfortable situations. Science fiction writer Frank Herbert, author of *Dune*, the best-selling science fiction novel of all time, understood this when he wrote "I must not fear. Fear is the mind-killer. Fear is the little death that brings total obliteration. I will face my fear. I will permit it to pass over me and through me. So that only I remain."[23] To help people get comfortable in uncomfortable situations, this section of the training program discussed traveling outside of life's comfort zone, outgrowing one's shoes, learning to manage fear, and navigating the intersection of fear and grit. This chapter provided numerous examples of how individuals were able to get comfortable in uncomfortable situations. These lessons are available to anyone willing to engage in the self-reflection, self-awareness, and self-care required to apply such experiences to the postpandemic world. This essential skill of getting comfortable in uncomfortable situations has been around for a long-time and will continue to serve as a viable option for those looking to embrace the ambiguity of the years ahead. Getting comfortable in uncomfortable situations can also help one practice the next essential skill of managing stress and anxiety.

Assessment: Open-Ended Questions

- How often are you traveling outside of your comfort zone?
- Do you believe the impossibly wonderful things are possible?
- How often do you allow yourself to outgrow your shoes?
- How often do you use fear as fuel to take you to the brink of not knowing what to do?
- How often do you use your uncomfortableness to challenge your attention and enhance your problem-solving skills?
- Has anyone ever mentioned that you should travel outside of your comfort zone? If so, how did you respond?
- Have you ever told anyone they should travel outside of their comfort zone? If so, how did they respond?
- Have you ever pushed past the pain of discomfort to achieve something you previously thought impossible?

Exercise: Inspirational Staircase

Directions: Using the inspirational staircase below, think about an accomplishment in your life. How many of these steps did you take on your path to accomplishing that goal? You can use this exercise for any number of accomplishments in your life.

```
                                        ┌─ I did it!
                                   ┌────┘
                                   │ I will do it.
                              ┌────┘
                              │ I will try to do it.
                         ┌────┘
                         │ How do I do it?
                    ┌────┘
                    │ I want to do it
               ┌────┘
               │ I can't do it
          ┌────┘
          │ I won't do it
```

Assessment: Comfort Zone Travels

- Directions: Determine how often you travel outside of your comfort zone, and out into the fear, learning, or growth zones by answering the following questions.
- During the pandemic, how frequently did you travel outside of your comfort zone? If you did, which zone did you travel to?
- For the year prior to the pandemic, how frequently did you travel outside of your comfort zone? If you did, which zone did you travel to?
- Five years ago, how frequently did you travel outside of your comfort zone? If you did, which zone did you travel to?
- For the next year, how often would you like to travel outside of your comfort zone? Why?

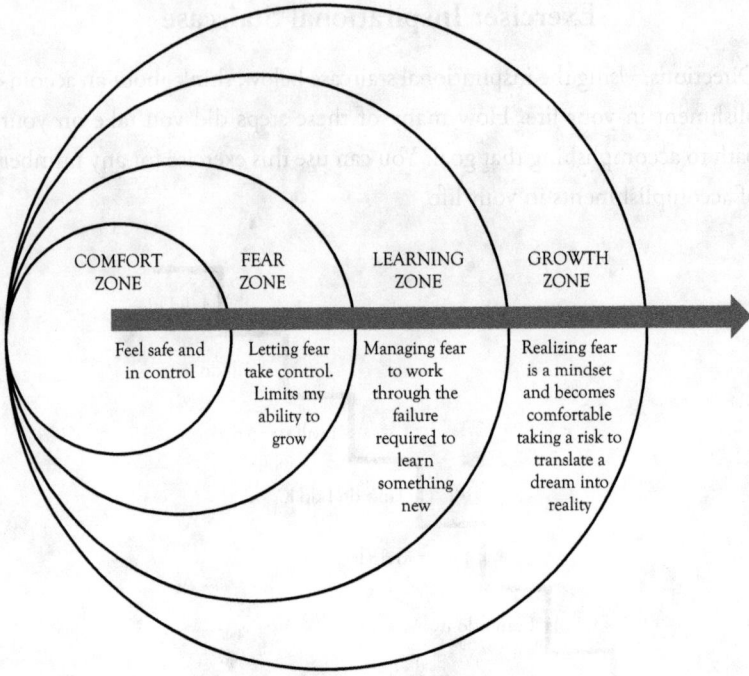

COMFORT ZONE	FEAR ZONE	LEARNING ZONE	GROWTH ZONE
Feel safe and in control	Letting fear take control. Limits my ability to grow	Managing fear to work through the failure required to learn something new	Realizing fear is a mindset and becomes comfortable taking a risk to translate a dream into reality

CHAPTER 13

Essential Skill 7: Manage Stress and Anxiety

To embrace the ambiguity of a postpandemic world, the seventh essential skill to develop is to manage stress and anxiety. Living and working through the COVID-19 global pandemic provided a year's worth of successive traumas. Mental health, already a national concern, rose in prominence as millions of people struggled to deal with the limitations, restrictions, and realities of living through a global pandemic. According to one study "anxiety and depression rates skyrocketed during the pandemic, with a 93 percent increase in people participating in anxiety screenings."[1] It would be difficult to find another abbreviated period of time where rates of mental health issues such as anxiety and depression increased at alarming rates. After such an extended period of turmoil, it is understandable why so many people are hesitant as to what comes next in the postpandemic VUCA world. As Dr. Aimee Daramus noted "It's understandable if people are anxious about what might happen next. It will take a while to believe that maybe this is the part of the story when things get better."[2] For many people living in a pandemic has become normalized. Moving forward in the postpandemic world, therefore, can add to life's uncertainty and can be, in the words of Dr. Carla Manly author of *Joy From Fear* "a substantial source of stress and anxiety since we have no idea what life will look like when the pandemic is over or whenever that day will be. The mere thought of yet another slew of changes is disconcerting."[3] To manage stress and anxiety, history provides evidence of the four strategies included in this section of the training program: learn how to manage fear, embrace excitement, remain graceful under pressure, and gather strength from distress.

The first strategy to practice the essential skill of managing stress and anxiety in the postpandemic world is learning how to manage fear. Now this is important; note the use of the word "manage" and not avoid, remove, or ignore. Since the absence of fear is nearly impossible learning to manage fear is a critical strategy, many people have used throughout history to help them manage stress and anxiety. Researchers continue to investigate the complexity of fear and its impact on humans in a variety of settings. One such researcher was Daniel Gardner who published the 2008 book *The Science of Fear: Why We Fear the Things We Shouldn't—and Put Ourselves in Greater Danger.* Gardner's research concluded "From terror attacks to the war on terror, real estate bubbles to the price of oil, to poisoned food from China, our list of fears is ever-growing. And yet, we are the safest and healthiest humans in history."[4] In his book Gardner included the work of Professor Gerd Gigerenzer, a German academic specializing in risk. In a 2004 article, Gigerenzer estimated an additional 1,595 Americans died in car accidents in the year after the 2001 terrorist attacks—indirect victims of the tragedy. He used trends in road and air use to suggest that, for a period of about 12 months, there was a temporary increase in road use before citizens again became more willing to fly at similar rates to before the attacks. Gigerenzer ascribed the extra deaths to a fear of dread risks, that is, low-probability, high-consequence events, such as the terrorist attack on September 11, 2001, and therefore, "people jumped from the frying pan into the fire."[5] Gigerenzer concluded that "informing the public about psychological research concerning dread risks could possibly save lives."[6] Doing so would go a long way helping people manage fear.

Another dynamic involved in managing fear to engage in the self-care required for mental health is Mark Twain's thought that "Courage is resistance to fear, mastery of fear—not absence of fear." Fear was rampant during the COVID-19 pandemic, and in some circles, it still remains. For those generally skeptical, the fear will persist in the postpandemic environment. With that in mind, Twain reminds people that fear will always exist, so it is important to learn how to master, or manage it. Do you have the courage required to manage fear? Mountain climber Emily Harrington did. In November 2020, Harrington became the first woman to free-climb El Capitan via Golden Gate, the 3,000 feet granite wall in Yosemite National Park in under 24 hours. Free climbing means the climber wears a rope to catch themselves, but they don't use any artificial means to help ascend the wall. This should not be confused with free soloing where the climber uses no ropes at all to catch themselves if they fall. Earlier this publication included the story of Alex Honnold, the only person to ever free-solo El Capitan. This section includes Harrington's story because she learned how to manage fear after suffering a serious accident years earlier. An attempt in 2019 ended in disaster after Harrington fell 50 feet, hit her head on a ledge, and suffered concussion. As she recalled "It was very scary. It was very serious initially and it turned out that I got lucky and did not suffer any long-term injuries. It's definitely a mental struggle, coming over that hurdle, coming back into this year and trying again."[7] During her climbing adventures, Harrington regularly feels fear. As Harrington said "We should be less afraid to be afraid. It's a very valid emotion and it's something we shouldn't shy away from. In a lot of ways, we can use it as fuel and as strength."[8] Harrington's observation provides a blueprint on how to manage fear:

- Acknowledge it exists.
- Accept it will continue to exist.
- Understand the goal is to be less afraid.
- Recognize it is a valid emotion.
- Realize there is no need to shy away from it.
- Use it as fuel and strength.

Embracing excitement is another strategy to practice the essential skill of managing stress and anxiety post pandemic. History has provided numerous examples of decision making under pressure. One's character is often defined by the decisions made. The global pandemic placed individuals from all walks of life across the globe under tremendous pressure. Truth be told, life placed pressure on people prior to the pandemic and will do so post pandemic as well. Life is stressful. Therefore, the more one can learn how to think differently about managing stress and anxiety using a technique known as reappraisal, the better their chances of embracing ambiguity. Reappraisal is nothing more than a cognitive process of going from a state of anxiety to a state of calmness. To see if this would work,

Harvard Business School professor Alison Wood Brooks designed an experiment to find out if telling people to calm down during a stressful moment was beneficial. In her research paper "Get Excited: Reappraising Pre-Performance Anxiety as Excitement," published in the *Journal of Experimental Psychology*, she recruited 140 people to give a speech. She told part of the group to relax and repeat the phrase "I am calm," while the others were told to embrace their anxiety and tell themselves, "I am excited." Members of both groups were still nervous before the speech, but the participants who had told themselves "I am excited" felt better able to handle the pressure, were more confident of their ability to give a compelling talk and received higher approval ratings from the audience.[9] The excited speakers were found to be more persuasive, confident, and competent than the participants who had tried to calm down. By changing the mindset just slightly, from "calm down" to "I am excited," the speakers engaged in the cognitive process that allowed them to transform their anxiety into energy that helped them to perform under pressure.

Another view of reappraisal allows the working definition to involve the "reframing of an emotional event in order to modulate one's experience of negative or positive emotion."[10] Thus, when someone alters their thinking about a stressful life situation, they are reappraising their emotions. As Brooks noted: "Individuals can reappraise anxiety as excitement using minimal strategies such as self-talk (e.g., saying "I am excited" out loud) or simple messages (e.g., "get excited"), which lead them to feel more excited, adopt an opportunity mind-set (as opposed to a threat mind-set), and improve their subsequent performance."[11] This reappraising approach can help individuals avoid choking, or failing, during a stressful event. In her book *Choke: What the Secrets of the Brain Reveal About Getting It Right When You Have To*, Sian Beilock, PhD, suggests that choking can occur when people think too much about activities that are usually automatic and suffer from "paralysis by analysis." Unfortunately, people also choke under pressure when they are not devoting enough attention to what they are doing and rely on simple or incorrect routines. For example, Professor Geir Jordet from the Norwegian School of Sports Sciences examined the pressure that soccer players face during penalty shots. Jordet examined the film footage of almost 400 kicks from penalty shootouts during major tournaments and found that players need to take their time.[12] Using the film footage, Jordet timed exactly how long players took to place the ball on the penalty spot. Those who took less than a second scored 58 percent of the time, compared with 80 percent when they didn't rush it and took longer than a second. Adjusting to the pressure of a penalty shot takes time, so players who adapt practice that habit.

A third strategy to practice the essential skill of managing stress and anxiety is to remain graceful under pressure. While reappraising one's approach toward a stressful situation involves a shift in cognitive functioning from "calm down" to "I'm excited," another dynamic also available to people is to remain graceful under pressure. Intense and stressful life situations are rarely scheduled, predetermined, or routine. In 1967, utility pole worker J.D. Thompson was working on a utility pole with his co-worker Randall Champion. The two power linemen were performing routine maintenance when one day Champion brushed one of the high-voltage lines at the very top of the utility pole. These are the lines that can be heard "singing" with electricity. Over 4,000 volts entered Champion's body and instantly stopped his heart (an electric chair uses about 2,000 volts). His safety harness prevented a fall, and Thompson, who had been ascending below him, quickly realized what happened and raced up the pole to perform mouth-to-mouth resuscitation. Thompson was unable to perform CPR given the circumstances but continued breathing into Champion's lungs until he felt a slight pulse, then unbuckled his harness and descended with him on his shoulder.[13] Thompson and another worker administered CPR on the ground, and Champion was moderately revived by the time paramedics arrived, eventually making a full recovery. The apprentice lineman exhibited tremendous courage, unwavering determination, and grace under extreme pressure to save a life. Champion lived another 35 years, surviving another electrical shock along the way, before dying of heart failure in 2002. Yet when you ask Thompson about the split second, he says he was just doing his job, following his training and that it was no big deal. Rocco Morabito took the photograph, entitled "The Kiss of Life," that would eventually win the 1968 Pulitzer Prize for Spot News Photography.[14]

Much like Thompson, professional baseball player Jim Rice demonstrated grace under pressure to save a life. During a Red Sox baseball game on August 8, 1982, a line drive struck 4-year-old Jonathan Keane in the side of the head. Recognizing that the boy needed immediate medical attention, Red Sox first basemen Rice went into the stands, picked up the boy and rushed him to the dugout where he received immediate medical attention. Newspaper photos from 1982, published in the *Boston Herald* and *Boston Globe*, show Boston Red Sox star Jim Rice carrying a badly injured little boy out of the stands moments after a ball hit him in the head. Within just a few minutes, Jonathan was rushed to the hospital where doctors credited Rice with saving the boy's life. Keane spent five days in the hospital in critical condition but returned to Fenway Park the following season to throw out the first pitch at opening day.[15] Keane is alive and well and has no recollection of how Rice stayed cool under pressure to save his life. "I think about my family and Jim Rice saving us, saving my life," he said. "Everyone else didn't do anything and he had that reaction … Instinctively lifted me out of the stands and bringing me to the ambulance."[16] Stories of grace under pressure remind us of what is possible, the depths of the human spirit, and the power of healing. As societies around the world emerge from the COVID-19 induced fog, people everywhere would serve themselves well by remembering the value of remaining graceful under pressure to embrace the ambiguity.

Gathering strength from distress is another strategy to practice the essential skill of managing stress and anxiety. For decades, soul singer Sharon Jones dealt with record label officials telling her she was "too short, too fat, too black and too old."[17] Jones was 40 years old when she was able to release her first record. In 2014, Jones was nominated for her first Grammy, in the category Best R&B Album, for *Give the People What They Want*. As children, she and her brothers would often imitate the singing and dancing of James Brown. A regular gospel singer in church, during the early 1970s, Jones often entered talent shows backed by local funk bands. Session work then continued with backing vocals but in the absence of any recording contract as a solo singer, she spent many years working as a corrections officer at Rikers Island and as an armored car guard for Wells Fargo, until receiving a mid-life career break in 1996 after she appeared on a session backing the soul and deep funk legend Lee Fields. Jones was the only one of three singers called to the session to show up. Having completed all the backing parts herself, Roth and Lehman were suitably impressed with her performance and recorded "Switchblade," a solo track with Jones. As a result of her performance, Jones would eventually be invited to join the Dap-Kings and in 2001, the band released *Dap Dippin' with Sharon Jones and the Dap-Kings*.[18] In 2015, a documentary titled *Miss Sharon Jones!* debuted at the Toronto International Film Festival.[19] The film depicts Jones's battle with cancer while continuing to perform. Sharon Jones died in 2016, with the band releasing the posthumous final album *Soul of a Woman* in 2017.

To manage stress and anxiety and embrace ambiguity in the post-pandemic environment, there are four strategies in this section of the training program to consider: learn how to manage fear, embrace excitement, remain graceful under pressure, and gather strength from distress. This chapter provided numerous examples of how individuals successfully navigated stressful life events. These lessons are available to anyone willing to engage in the self-reflection, self-awareness, and self-care required to apply such experiences to the postpandemic world. Much work remains to be done, however, as stress and anxiety rates are still high. The *2021 Emerging from the Pandemic Survey* noted this continued trend of mental health concerns, published in February 2021 by the firm Willis Towers Watson, and noted that employers' biggest well-being challenges are rising stress and burnout, increased caregiving demands, and decreased social connections.[20] Thus, this essential skill of managing stress and anxiety has been around for a long-time and will continue to serve as a viable option for those looking to embrace the ambiguity of the years ahead. American political journalist and world peace advocate Norman Cousins noted "History is a vast early warning system."[21] By leveraging the lessons from those who successfully manages their stress and anxiety, this component of the training program serves as an extension of that early warning system and involves the following set of questions and assessments. Managing stress and anxiety can also help one practice the next essential skill of understanding the role of nuance in decision making.

Assessment: Open-Ended Questions

- Do you believe "the harder the conflict, the more glorious the triumph?"
- Do you believe "what we obtain too cheap, we esteem too lightly?"

- How often have you smiled in trouble?
- Have often do you gather strength from distress?
- How often do you grow brave by reflection?
- How often is your heart firm?
- How often do you pursue your principles?
- How often do you acknowledge fear exists?
- How often do you accept fear will continue to exist?
- How often do you understand the goal is to be less afraid?
- How often do you recognize fear is a valid emotion?
- How often do you realize there is no need to shy away from fear?
- How often do you use fear as fuel and strength?

Assessment: Anxiety and Stress Management Checklist

Directions: Review the 12-option checklist to manage anxiety and stress and mark each one that you use for each day. See if you can complete this exercise for an entire week to track your progress. You can always make copies of this checklist to trend your activity over longer periods of time.

Stress and Anxiety Management Weekly Checklist							
Option	M	T	W	TH	F	SA	SU
Choose 'progress over perfection' mindset							
Maintain a positive attitude							
Identify your triggers							
Accept you cannot control everything							
Get enough sleep							
Look away from all electronic devices & screens							
Take a walk outside or exercise							
Be sure to eat well							
Slowly count to 10							
Volunteer in your community							
Meditate or take daily time outs							
Talk to someone							

Exercise: Managing Your Fear

Directions: Using Harrington's observation, we have a blueprint on how to manage fear. Think of a life situation that invoked fear for you. Did you use any of the tactics Harrington used to manage fear? Write your answers in the space after each step in the process.

Life situation_____

Harrington's Six Steps to Manage Fear

1. Acknowledge it exists.
2. Accept it will continue to exist.
3. Understand the goal is to be less afraid.
4. Recognize it is a valid emotion.
5. There is no need to shy away from it.
6. Use it as fuel and strength.

CHAPTER 14

Essential Skill 8: Understand the Role of Nuance

Recognizing the nuance involved with decision making is the eighth essential skill to develop for those interested in embracing the ambiguity of a postpandemic world. The definition of nuance means "slight or delicate degree of difference in expression, feeling, or opinion." The etymology of the word echoes back to the 18th century from the French "nuance" meaning "slight difference, shade of color, or shades" and from the Latin "nubes" meaning "a cloud, mist, or vapor." Nuance has been commonly used when referring to the different shapes, sizes, and colors of the clouds. When discussing, assessing, and thinking about political or social issues, remember the origin of the word nuance involves the complex characteristics involved with cloud. Clouds are not binary; just as no political or social issue is. Clouds are complex, multidimensional, and elaborate and are given different names based on their shape and their height in the sky. Most clouds can be divided into groups (high/ middle/low) based on the height of the cloud's base above the Earth's surface. Other clouds are grouped but by their unique characteristics, such as forming alongside mountains (Lenticular clouds) or forming beneath existing clouds (Mammatus clouds). The postpandemic issues individuals, organizations, and societies around the world will need to address are just as complex as clouds. This has been true, however, for most of history. Life is far more complex than the typical binary approach people use to think about an issue. For example, the "winners never quit" belief demonstrates a simplistic approach that fails to consider the nuance involved with the decision-making process. Winners quit all the time. Winners quit smoking. Winners quit stop making excuses. Winners get themselves out of terrible relationships. Winners leave their comfort zone. "Winners never quit" is merely one of the many examples of nuance. To understand the role of nuance in the decision-making process, history provides evidence of the four strategies included in this section of the training program: assess your decision-making process, decide if you are going to leave, chance, or accept your situation, observe your reaction, and recognize the space between stimulus and response.

The first strategy to practice the essential skill of understanding the role of nuance is to assess your decision-making process. Making decisions is a daily occurrence for those who navigate the chaos and practice the art of living well. In his 2013 book *How to Fail at Almost Everything and Still Win Big: Kind of the Story of My Life*, cartoonist and author Scott Adams highlights two important aspects of his success: "Good ideas have no value because the world already has too many of them. The market rewards execution, not ideas," and "Goals are for losers. Focus on the process."[1] In the postpandemic environment, remaining focused on goals is certainly a critical component of embracing the ambiguity. When assessing your decision-making process related to goals, remember what Bryan Collins wrote in *Forbes* "If the goal is particularly difficult to achieve, working on it without seeing tangible progress induces feelings of stress. You also might not be able to control the outcome of a goal because of changing circumstances."[2] For example, just think about all those personal and professional goals the pandemic derailed. For those who were goal-oriented prior to the pandemic, Adams would describe them "in a state of continuous pre-success failure at best, and permanent failure at worst if things never work out." For those willing to change, however, and switch their decision-making process then "systems people succeed every time they apply their systems, in the sense that they did what they intended to do."[3]

One person who developed an efficient system-based decision-making model was Dwight D. Eisenhower. In a 1954 speech to the Second Assembly of the World Council of Churches, U.S. President Dwight D. Eisenhower said: "I have two kinds of problems: the urgent and the important. The urgent are not important, and the important are never urgent."[4] Often referred to as the "Eisenhower Principle" on organizing workload and priorities this decision-making process involves a 2×2 grid consisting of four categories:

- Urgent and important (tasks you will do immediately)
  DO IT.
- Important, but not urgent (tasks you will schedule to do later)
  DEFER IT.
- Urgent, but not important (tasks delegated to someone else)
  DELEGATE IT.
- Neither urgent nor important (tasks that you will eliminate)
  DELETE IT.

Also known as the 4 D approach to decision making: do it, defer it, delegate it, or delete it, Eisenhower's approach can help one understand that great time management means being effective as well as efficient.[5] It is important on both the personal and professional levels to prioritize spending time on those tasks that fall into the important and urgent categories. In the postpandemic VUCA world, leveraging a system-based decision-making process can help one better understand the nuance involved with answering questions, solving problems, and addressing issues.

Decide if you are going to leave, change, or accept your situation is another strategy to practice the essential skill of understanding the role of nuance. The pandemic provided workers across a spectrum of jobs, industries, and positions with a long period of time to reflect upon their life situation. Many workers asked themselves if they were going to leave, change, or accept their life situation. Leaving a place of employment is often difficult and might involve risk one is unable to or uncomfortable taking at that time for any number of reasons. Leaving and changing one's life situation is filled with nuance and requires one to think through the issues, questions, and concerns related to moving forward. Patience is required. As previously discussed, many people have used the pandemic to rethink their career trajectory. According to David Cathey, a partner with recruiting company Unity Search Group, "the nation's workforce is right at the beginning of a tsunami of people changing jobs. Since September 2020 we have had consecutive job order growth month over month and it's only increasing. We're not seeing that slow down."[6] This "tsunami" of turnover in the workforce is a direct result of the reflection people engaged in during the pandemic. As Cathey noted the time at home during the pandemic allowed workers to opportunity to contemplate their situation and man "found out is that life is short, and they really want to be satisfied with the work that they're doing and the company that they are working for."[7]

One such example in history of someone who decided to change his situation was Bill Nunn, sports editor at *The Pittsburgh Courier*, an African American newspaper that covered sports at black college. Beginning in 1950, the paper named a black college all-American football team. By the late 1960s, Nunn was frustrated that National Football League teams had not drafted more of the players his paper honored. When he shared his feelings with Dan Rooney, the son of the Steelers' owner, Art Rooney, he did not get an argument—the Steelers hired him. Nunn began working for the team part time in 1967 and became full time in 1969, the year Chuck Noll became the coach. Over the next decade, Nunn helped steer the team toward many players who went on to star for the Steelers teams that won four Super Bowls from 1975 to 1980. Among them were John Stallworth (Alabama A&M), L. C. Greenwood (Arkansas-Pine Bluff), Mel Blount (Southern), Dwight White (East Texas State), Donnie Shell (South Carolina State), and Ernie Holmes (Texas Southern). Mel Blount said, "When you look at the Steelers of the 1970s, none of that would have happened without Bill Nunn."[8] Nunn did not use an excuse and instead, found a way to change the way the NFL recruited African American players.

In his best-selling book *The Power of Now*, Eckert Tolle challenged the reader to reflect upon their level of complaining about their life situation. Did they complain out loud to someone else, to themselves, or both? Armed with that self-awareness, Tolle then made the following observation about leaving, changing, or accepting one's life situation "To complain is nonacceptance of what is. When you complain, you make yourself into a victim. So, change the situation by acting or by speaking out if necessary or possible; leave the situation or accept it. All else is madness."[9] Do you understand the nuances involved with changing your life situation? Have you spent enough time reflecting upon how to leave, change, or accept your life situation? History has demonstrated that people realize this "madness" and leave their jobs when their level of unhappiness is coupled with the existence of available positions. For example, in 2019, workers were quitting their jobs at record rates, with labor experts saying workers did so in order to secure better pay and positions. As the postpandemic VUCA marketplace emerges, workers are likely to seek new employment opportunities as some estimates suggest 25 percent of workers are looking for new opportunities.[10]

A third strategy to practice the essential skill of understanding the role of nuance is to observe your reaction. This is a challenging question because it shifts the responsibility away from the situation and onto the individual. It is far easier for the individual to blame a situation instead of recognizing they have the strength, courage, and ability to create a more intentional reaction. Observing one's reaction, and responding with intention, however, is difficult since ego often interferes. Many people lack the self-awareness to set their ego aside to determine the best course of action. To that end, clinical psychologist Dr. Leslie Becker-Phelps suggests four strategies to use. First, before responding, an individual should envision the person they would like to be and react in the manner appropriate for such a vision. Before reacting, the individual should pause for a moment and remind themselves of who they would like to be and how they would like to respond. Second, before responding, an individual should set aside time to think about the meaning or origin of their reactions. Such reflection allows one to better understand the myriad of other factors unrelated to the situation yet are impacting their reaction. Emotions, stress, and fear often create hurdles to responding with intention. Third, those who wish to observe their reaction and respond with intentional should pay close attention to the results of their reactions. By increasing their awareness of the consequences of their reactions, one can better position themselves to respond with intention. Finally, individuals should consider practicing a more compassionate approach to responding to people, situations, and events. Doing so has the byproduct of exercise the self-care often required. As Dr. Becker-Phelps suggested, "personal change takes effort and time to accomplish; being critical towards yourself will only undermine your efforts."[11]

One lesson from history included in this training program stems from actor Mariska Hargitay who worked intentionally on her reaction when she got rejected for the show *ER*. She prepared so well for her audition; the casting agent said she was too good for the role. Instead of blaming the casting director, she leveraged her connections, did not take no for an answer, and went the extra mile to explain why she was the right actress for the role. It worked. Her work on *ER* helped launch Mariska's career where she would eventually go on to star in *Law and Order: Special Victims Unit* for over 20 seasons. She could have easily moved on to the next audition; or she could have reacted in a negative manner. Instead, she tempered her reaction and in so doing altered her career trajectory. As Brazilian author Paulo Coelho noted "Your problem isn't the problem. Your reaction is the problem."[12] Embracing the ambiguity of the postpandemic VUCA world will demand an acceptance of this very fact—your reaction is the problem. Those who react with anger, bitterness, or closed-mindedness lack any ability to react with intention. When that happens, the person who should be responding with intention is allowing the situation, or perhaps someone else, to control how they react. It is important to remember that how one reacts, or does not react, is an action onto itself. Therefore, in the postpandemic VUCA environment, one should consider asking themselves how often they want to let other people or events control their response or the direction of their life.

Recognizing the space between stimulus and response is another strategy to practice the essential skill of understanding the role of nuance. In the postpandemic VUCA world, with the dynamics of living and working changing with such high frequency, it will be important to understand how patience is an acquired trait. That is, one can actually practice being patient. Patience is available to anyone willing to put in the time, effort, and practice. Such learned behavior comes from reflection, self-awareness, and SDL assessments and questions like those posed at the end of this chapter. As life gets ever more complicated, learning how to recognize the space between stimulus and response will be an important strategy to consider using for anyone looking to embrace the ambiguity of the postpandemic world. Remember, this training program is built on the belief that the only thing one can truly change is their own self. As Gregory L. Jantz wrote "Patience allows you to take back control over the capricious and unstable world and plant that control firmly within yourself. Patience does not give you the power over circumstances; patience allows you to control yourself in the midst of circumstances."[13] From an historical perspective, one such person who has advocated that people recognize the space between stimulus and response is best-selling author Stephen Covey.

In 1969, Covey was on sabbatical from Brigham Young University to write a book. While wandering through the stacks of a university library in Hawaii one came across the following passage "Between stimulus and response, there is a space. In that space is our power to choose our response. In our response lies our growth and our freedom." This quote is often attributed to Viktor E. Frankl but there is no direct evidence he ever wrote those lines. An examination into the originations of the quote suggest Covey may have been reading an article by the influential psychologist Rollo May. Nevertheless, that passage "Between stimulus and response, there is a space. In that space is our power to choose our response. In our response lies our growth and our freedom." altered Covey's life approach. Those three lines would eventually form the foundation for his book, *The 7 Habits of Highly Effective People,* first published in 1989.[14] History provides countless examples of people who measured their response in a crisis. One such example is Katharine Graham.

Graham, president, and publisher of *The Washington Post* during the 1970s and 1980s, demonstrated a measured approach to responding to one crisis after another. Whether it was publishing stories related to unveiling the Watergate conspiracy, that ultimately led to the resignation of President Richard Nixon, or the publication of the Pentagon Papers, detailing U.S. involvement in Vietnam, Graham time and again took one risk after another after recognizing the space between stimulus and response and leveraged her resolve to elevate her paper and the state of journalism. Graham could have easily had a response of hiding in the shadows, bowing to the pressure to not print such volatile information, or burying her head in the sand ignoring such high-profile stories. She did none of that and instead responded by publishing the Pentagon Papers and Watergate stories and in so doing would make the *Washington Post* the most famous newspaper on the planet.[15] Insight into the nuance involved with her decision-making process came in the form of November 16, 1988, speech while presenting at the CIA headquarters as part of that agency's Office of Training and Education's Guest Speaker series. In discussing the potential for press disclosures to affect national security, Graham said: "We live in a dirty and dangerous world. There are some things the general public does not need to know and shouldn't. I believe democracy flourishes when the government can take legitimate steps to keep its secrets and when the press can decide whether to print what it knows."[16] Graham's career also exemplifies how, as Nancy Koehn wrote "real leaders are not born." For Koehn, real leaders like Graham develop an ability to help others triumph over adversity. Such insight is not written into their genetic code. Koehn acknowledged that "real leaders are made when they are forged in crisis. Leaders become 'real' whey they practice a few key behaviors that gird and inspire people through difficult times."[17]

To understand the role of nuance in the postpandemic world, there are four strategies in this section of the training program: assess your decision-making process; decide if you are going to leave, chance, or accept your situation; observe your reaction; and recognize the space between stimulus and response. Lesley Candace Visser understood the value of nuance in navigating her career in becoming the first female NFL analyst on TV, and the only sportscaster in history (male or female) who has worked on Final Four, NBA Finals, World Series, Triple Crown, Monday Night Football, the Olympics, the Super Bowl, the World Figure Skating Championships, and the U.S. Open network broadcasts. Visser, who was voted the No. 1 Female Sportscaster of all-time in a poll taken by the American Sportscasters Association, was elected to the National Sportscasters and Sportswriters Association's Hall of Fame in 2015. When Lesley was 11, she told her mother that she wanted to be a sportswriter. The job didn't exist for women in 1964, but her mother—instead of suggesting she become a teacher or a nurse—replied, "Great! Sometimes you have to cross when it says, 'Don't walk.'" That answer changed Lesley's life. Even though no one had done it before, it gave her the strength and self-confidence to try—permission to cross against the light. Her mother's advice would eventually become the title of Visser's 2017 autobiography *Sometimes You Have to Cross When It Says Don't Walk: A Memoir of Breaking Barriers.* By heeding her mother's advice and walking across the street when the sign says "don't walk," Visser allowed her story to exemplify the next essential skill of remaining open to the unfolding of life.

Assessment: Open-Ended Questions

- How often do you reflect upon nuance?
- How often do you listen to opinions completely different from your own to engage in the hard work required to reflect upon nuance?
- How often do you force your opinions on others without any consideration of the nuances involved?
- How often do you engage in the slight difference involved with a topic, issue, or concern?
- When you examine the clouds do you accept how different they all are?
- Do you apply that same level of understanding in other aspects of your life?
- How often in a day do you catch yourself complaining aloud?
- How often in a day do you catch yourself complaining in thought?
- How often do you find yourself in a state of nonacceptance?
- What have you done lately to change or leave your state of nonacceptance?
- Do you maintain the self-awareness required to understand if you carry, in Tolle's words, "an unconscious negative charge"?
- How often do you make yourself the victim?
- Have you forgotten your ability to leave or change a situation?
- Are you making excuses as to why you are unable to leave or change a situation?
- Do you just complain and never make any effort to leave or change your life situation? In other words, just how mad are you?
- How often do you recognize the space between stimulus and response?
- How comfortable you are crossing the street when the sign says, "don't walk"?

Exercise: Time to Respond

Directions: Think of a life situation where there was a stimulus and your response. Write your responses to the following questions to identify your time to response.

Life situation_____

- Did you recognize the space between stimulus and response?
- Did you understand in that space is your power to choose your response?
- Did you acknowledge that in your response lies your growth and your freedom?
- Did you measure your time to respond to the stimulus in this life situation?
- Did you use the strategy of "counting to 10" to respond?
- Did you tell someone you needed to "sleep on it" before responding?
- Did you respond hastily and then regret doing so?

Assessment: The 2×2 Decision-Making Matrix

Directions: Using the following Eisenhower Decision-Making Matrix, also known as the 4D approach, write down 20 items on your to do list and place each task in one of the four categories.

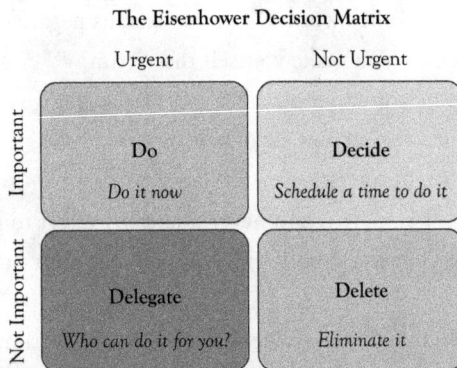

The Eisenhower Decision Matrix

	Urgent	Not Urgent
Important	**Do** *Do it now*	**Decide** *Schedule a time to do it*
Not Important	**Delegate** *Who can do it for you?*	**Delete** *Eliminate it*

Task	Category	Task	Category

CHAPTER 15

Essential Skill 9: Remain Open to the Unfolding of Life

To embrace the ambiguity of a postpandemic world, the ninth essential skill to develop is to remain open to the unfolding of life. "In the face of dire economic uncertainty, layoffs, and swirling cyclones of conflicting information, people are fearful, and leaders understandably want to allay those fears."[1] As Ron Carucci wrote in *Forbes*, one way to help yourself and others during periods of uncertainty is to extend "an invitation to discover hope."[2] History has proven time and again that to invite hope is to remain open to the unfolding of life. *New York Times* editorialist David Brooks wrote about the potential of life's unfolding when he observed how people are terrible at imagining how they will feel in the future and exaggerate how much the future will resemble the present. Since the capacity for imagining the future are bad in normal times, Brooks noted "they are horrible in moments of stress and suffering."[3] Given these weaknesses, Brooks suggested "it seems wrong to make a decision that will foreclose future thinking. It seems wrong to imagine you have mastery over your feelings and thoughts. It's better to respect the future and remain humbly open to your own unfolding."[4] In 1997, British author Stephen Batchelor published *Buddhism Without Beliefs: A Contemporary Guide to Awakening* and challenged the reader to think about three different, yet related aspects of life's unfolding. First, the global population resembles a "vast musical instrument on which we play our individual part while simultaneously listening to the compositions of others to contribute to the whole. We don't choose whether to engage, only how to; we either harmonize or create dissonance."[5] Second, Batchelor stressed how people need to pay attention to their words and deeds since "our very presence creates and leaves impressions in the minds of others just as a writer makes impressions with their words."[6] Finally, he challenged the reader to remember that "Who you are is an unfolding narrative. You came from nothing and will return there eventually. Instead of taking ourselves so seriously all the time, we can discover the playful irony of a story that has never been told in quite this way before."[7] To remain open to the unfolding of life, history provides evidence of the four strategies included in this section of the training program: think about your three possible selves, set aside your ego, stay true to yourself, and take care of your own grass.

The first strategy to practice the essential skill of remaining open to the unfolding of life is to think about your three possible selves. The work of Hazel Rose Markus and Paula Nurius introduced the concept of three possible selves in a paper published in 1986: the ideal self that we would like to become, that we could become, and that we are afraid of becoming. "To suggest that there is a single self to which one 'can be true' or an authentic self that one can know is to deny the rich network of potential that surrounds individuals."[8] The researchers discuss how the three possible selves are the cognitive components of hopes, fears, goals, and threats while also functioning as incentives for future behavior. In her 1968 publication, *Slouching Towards Bethlehem* author Joan Didion reflected upon the search for herself and said, "I have already lost touch with a couple of people I used to be." In her preface to the book, Didion writes, "I was paralyzed by the conviction that writing was an irrelevant act, that the world as I had understood it no longer existed. If I was to work again at all, it would be necessary for me to come to terms with disorder."[9] This historical reference, like the others included throughout this book, demonstrate that the ability to embrace ambiguity has been a prat of the human experience for quite some time. Author Lewis Carroll echoed similar sentiment and noted "It's no use going back to yesterday, because I was a different person then."[10] What a beautiful sentiment! Both Didion and Carroll experienced the transformation, maturation, and disorder related to the development of their "self" over time. They understood how their lives unfolded over time and they developed a new self. The backstories of actors Robert Downey Jr., Daniel Radcliffe, and Danny Trejo each provide an historical lesson and exemplify people who "lost touch with who they used to be."

Downey engaged in hard partying, reckless behavior, and drug use. He would eventually spend time in jail and rehab; two events that would spell the end of most careers. For Downey, however, he was cast on the television show *Ally McBeal* seven days after leaving rehab. Billed as the ultimate comeback, the once golden boy of Hollywood was ready to show the world he was a changed man. For a while, it worked as he helped increased the show's ratings. But he continued his previous ways, got arrested two more times, fired from *Ally McBeal*, and hit rock bottom. For the second time in his career, he began to tackle his demons. Unfortunately, his legal and drug issues prevented him from getting insurance as an actor. With help from his now wife Susan Levin, and Mel Gibson who cast Downey in a small movie and put himself on the line to get Downey insured, Downey's second personal turnaround succeeded. Between 2003 and 2008, Downey appeared in a variety of movies demonstrating to Hollywood that he was reliable and clean for good. In 2008 he appeared in his first *Iron Man* film, which would become a blockbuster.[11] By 2015, he was one of the industry's highest paid actors.

Daniel Radcliffe is best known for playing Harry Potter in the *Harry Potter* film series during his adolescence and early adulthood. He has been outspoken about his battle against alcohol addiction throughout much of his adult career. According to Radcliffe, "A lot of drinking that happened toward the end of Potter and for a little bit after it finished, it was panic, a little bit not knowing what to do next—not being comfortable enough in who I was to remain sober."[12] Sober since 2010, Radcliffe pulled himself out of the darkness of alcohol abuse with the help of close friends, who genuinely cared for his well-being and offered great advice. Upon reflection he said "It took a few years, and it took a couple of attempts. Ultimately, it was my own decision. ... I woke up one morning after a night going, 'This is probably not good.'"[13]

Throughout the 1960s, Danny Trejo was in and out of jail and prison in California. He has suggested his physical appearance contributed to his constantly getting into trouble. While serving in San Quentin, he became a champion boxer in that prison's lightweight and welterweight divisions. During this time, Trejo became a member of a 12-step program, which he credits with his success in overcoming drug addiction. In 2011, he recalled that he had been sober for 42 years. While Trejo was working as a youth drug counselor, a teenage patient asked for his assistance dealing with cocaine problems on the set of *Runaway Train* (1985).[14] While there, Trejo was offered a job as an extra in the film's prison scenes. Edward Bunker, himself an individual who was formerly incarcerated and at the time a well-respected crime author who was writing the screenplay for the film, recognized Trejo, with whom he had done time at San Quentin and offered him $320 per day to train Eric Roberts, one of the movie's stars, for a boxing scene. Director Andrei Konchalovsky liked Trejo's work and decided to offer him a small role in the film as a boxer.

Setting aside your ego is another strategy to practice the essential skill of remaining open to the unfolding of life. This second strategy of setting aside your ego is linked to the previous one of thinking about your three possible selves. Ego refers to the Latin and ancient Greek word for "I." Yes, of course, there are those who achieve success and have tremendous egos. They use "I" incessantly. In their writing, their speeches, and their interactions with others, it is always about them, and their ego. Sadly, even those who have yet to accomplish much at all can have a tendency to exhibit an overinflated ego. On the role of ego author Eckhart Tolle wrote in his 2005 publication *A New Earth: Awakening to Your Life's Purpose* "I have met people who may be technically good at what they do but whose ego constantly sabotages their work. Only part of their attention is on the work they perform; the other part is on themselves."[15] Doing so, however, prohibits them from setting aside their ego since they obsess with turning their attention inward at the expense of ignoring their world. Tolle explained how, for these people, "their ego demands personal recognition and wastes energy in resentment if it doesn't get enough, or if their focus of attention is profit or power, and their work is no more than a means to that end."[16] One person who put his ego aside to conduct high-quality work was Alex Trebek.

Trebek was a Canadian American game show host and television personality. He was the host of the syndicated game show *Jeopardy!* for 37 seasons from its revival in 1984 until his death in 2020. He would receive the Daytime Emmy Award for Outstanding Game Show Host seven times for his work on Jeopardy! He died on November 8, 2020, at age 80 after a nearly two-year battle with pancreatic cancer. Unlike many celebrities who conceal illness, Trebek was transparent about what he was going through. In a May 2019 interview on CBS's *Sunday Morning*, he said "Sometimes the pain would shoot from a three to an 11. I taped the show, and then I made it to the dressing room on one occasion, just barely, before I writhed in pain and cried in pain."[17] In March 2020, he gave a one-year video update on his status, noting that just 18 percent of people with pancreatic cancer live that long. "There were moments of great pain, days when certain bodily functions no longer functioned and sudden, massive attacks of great depression that made me wonder if it really was worth fighting on. But to give up would have been to betray loved ones who were helping me survive." Reflecting on his 37 seasons with *Jeopardy!* and his role as host, Trebek said "You have to set your ego aside. If you want to be a good host, you have to figure out a way to get the contestants to perform at their best. Because if they do well, the show does well. And if the show does well, by association, I do well."[18]

A third strategy to practice the essential skill of remaining open to the unfolding of life is to stay true to yourself. Eighteenth century Austrian composer Wolfgang Amadeus Mozart noted "I pay no attention whatever to anybody's praise or blame. I simply follow my own feelings."[19] One such example from recent history stems from the time when Irwin Winkler and Robert Chartoff offered Sylvester Stallone $350,000 for the rights to his script about a Philadelphia boxer but had their own casting ideas for the lead role, including Robert Redford and Burt Reynolds. Stallone, staying true to himself, refused to sell unless he played the lead character. Eventually, after a substantial budget cut to compromise, it was agreed he could be the star. Despite being nearly homeless and almost completely out of money, Stallone stayed true to himself and turned down the $350,000 to play the lead in the film *Rocky*, which would go on to become one of the most iconic movies of all time.[20] Stallone followed his own feelings, decided to lose in the short run to win in the long-run financially, and remained true to himself despite needing the money offered to him.

Researcher and author Brené Brown has spent a good deal of time examining this topic of being true to one's self. One reason some individuals lack a sense of their true self is because they are listening to the wrong people. As Brown wrote in *Rising Strong: How the Ability to Reset*

Transforms the Way We Live, Love, Parent, and Lead "A lot of cheap seats in the arena are filled with people who never venture onto the floor. They just hurl mean-spirited criticisms and put-downs from a safe distance."[21] To ignore what people think, however, creates the unintended consequence of disconnecting from them. On the other hand, when people let the words of others define who they are, people lose "the courage to be vulnerable. Therefore, we need to be selective about the feedback we let into our lives. For me, if you are not in the arena getting your ass kicked, I'm not interested in your feedback."[22] Brown brings up a good point. Why would you ever listen to someone who has never taken a risk in their life? To use her words, "if they are not getting their ass kicked," what might they have to offer you? Are you listening to everyone's criticism of your life situation? Why is that? To be true to your self requires one to exercise discernment between those who have earned the ability to criticize you and those who have not. Those closest to you who have earned such a place in the development of yourself, can provide the catalyst you need to develop. As author Shannon L. Alder wrote "Every woman that finally figured out her worth, has picked up her suitcases of pride and boarded a flight to freedom, which landed in the valley of change."[23] Who has helped you figure out your worth? Who has helped pilot your plane to the valley of change?

One such woman who remained true to herself, was American athlete Mildred Ella "Babe" Didrikson Zaharias. Zaharias was an American athlete ignored the critics and achieved a great deal of success in golf, basketball, baseball, and track and field. She won two gold medals in track and field at the 1932 Summer Olympics, before turning to professional golf and winning 10 LPGA major championships. She was named the 10th Greatest North American Athlete of the 20th Century by ESPN and the ninth Greatest Athlete of the 20th Century by the Associated Press.[24] In 1957, she posthumously received the Bob Jones Award, the highest honor given by the U.S. Golf Association in recognition of distinguished sportsmanship in golf. It was accepted by her husband George, four months after her death. She was one of six initial inductees into the LPGA Hall of Fame at its inception in 1977. Zaharias broke the accepted models of femininity in her time, including the accepted models of female athleticism. Standing 5 feet 7 inches tall and weighing 115 pounds, Zaharias was physically strong and socially straightforward about her strength. Although a sports hero to many, she was also derided for her "manliness." Babe performed at a time when female athletes were considered freakish at best, downright unacceptable at worst. For most of her life she was the antithesis of femininity; not until her later years did she dress and act less manly. "She was not a feminist, not a militant, not a strategist launching campaigns against sexual liberation," wrote William Johnson and Nancy Williamson in *Whatta-Gal!: The Babe Didrikson Story.* "She was an athlete, and her body was her most valuable possession." Some writers condemned her for not being feminine. "It would be much better if she and her ilk stayed at home, got themselves prettied up and waited for the phone to ring," Joe Williams wrote in the *New York World-Telegram.*[25]

Taking care of your own grass is another strategy to practice the essential skill of remaining open to the unfolding of life. If the grass is greener on the neighbor's lawn, did you ever stop to ask if they take better care of it? Are you so obsessed with the shade of green of other lawns you completely forget to take care of your own? The essential skill of remaining open to the unfolding of life reminds us to take care of our own lawn and commit to lifelong learning. As the 16th century French writer Michel de Montaigne noted, "There is nothing more notable in Socrates than that he found time, when he was an old man, to learn music and dancing, and thought it time well spent."[26] One example from history illustrating the strategy of taking care of your own grass to embrace life's ambiguity comes from actor Aaron Eckhert. After graduating from Brigham Young University in 1994 with a Bachelor of Fine Arts degree in film, Eckhert lived in New York City as a struggling, unemployed actor for several years. As an undergraduate at BYU, Eckhart met director and writer Neil LaBute, who cast him in several of his own original plays. Five years later, Eckhart made a debut as an unctuous, sociopathic ladies' man in LaBute's black comedy film *In the Company of Men* (1997). Under LaBute's guidance, he worked in the director's films *Your Friends & Neighbors* (1998). Eckhart would gain some recognition as George in Steven Soderbergh's critically acclaimed film *Erin Brockovich* (2000) but it was not until six years later, in 2006, that he received a Golden Globe nomination for his portrayal of Nick Naylor in *Thank You for Smoking.*

In an interview, actor Aaron Eckhert said, "You always have to go out there and prove yourself to people. It never ends. That's an important lesson No matter what level you are at. Never give up." Eckhert noted that "for 20 years I've made mistakes and recovered from mistakes. I have asked myself tough questions. I've just tried to be a better person, and not take everything so seriously."[27]

Much like Eckhert, professional tennis player Roger Federer has learned the value of self-improvement. Federer is ranked world No. 4 in men's singles tennis by the Association of Tennis Professionals. He has won 20 Grand Slam singles titles—the most in history for a male player—and has held the world No. 1 spot in the ATP rankings for a record total of 310 weeks (including a record 237 consecutive weeks) and was the year-end No. 1 five times. Federer, who turned professional in 1998, was continuously ranked in the top 10 from October 2002 to November 2016. Federer has won a record eight Wimbledon men's singles titles, six Australian Open titles, five U.S. Open titles (all consecutive, a record), and one French Open title. He is one of eight men to have achieved a Career Grand Slam. Federer has reached a record 31 men's singles Grand Slam finals, including 10 consecutively from the 2005 Wimbledon Championships to the 2007 U.S. Open. To remain at the top of his game for such an extended period of time, Federer relied upon the strategy of making sure his grass was always green. He always questioned himself, even in the best of times. As Federer recalled in an interview "when I was world number one for many, many weeks and months in a row, at certain times during the year I said, 'What can I improve? What do I need to change?'" These questions are critical for anyone working toward embracing the ambiguity of the situation. If one fails to ask such questions, however, they risk repeating the same mistakes over multiple times. Ultimately, one can wind up stumbling backwards. For Federer it was "important for me to actually hear criticism sometimes because I think that's what makes me a better player and that means someone's questioning me who really cares about me, and I think that's really important in the business world as well."[28]

To remain open to the unfolding of life there are four strategies in this section of the training program: think about your three possible selves, set aside your ego, stay true to yourself, and take care of your own grass.

Joseph Campbell noted "We must be willing to let go of the life we've planned so as to have the life that is waiting for us." First, one needs to "let go" which in and of itself it extremely difficult for anyone to do. Letting go of anything presents one of humanity's biggest challenges. Second, and a continuation of the first "let go of the life we have planned." If you have planned your life you are one of the fortunate ones as most people lack any sense of how or what to plan. But know that you have created a life plan, you need to let go of it. Finally, you need to remain "open to the life that is waiting for you." So, this last idea involves three different elements: a belief that a better life is even possible for you, an understanding that your current life situation could be improved, and an acceptance that your plans can evolve over time. Such was the case with Richard George Adams. While driving his daughters to school, Adams created a story about two young rabbits escaping from their doomed warren. Over time his daughters coaxed him into writing the story known as *Watership Down*.

Adams began writing in the evenings, and after two years he produced an exquisitely written story about a group of young rabbits escaping from their doomed warren. "It was rather difficult to start with. I was 52 when I discovered I could write. I wish I'd known a bit earlier. I never thought of myself as a writer until I became one."[29] Adams never thought of himself as a writer until he became one. He remained open to his life as a writer, even though it was difficult to work. The book gained international acclaim almost immediately for reinvigorating anthropomorphic fiction with naturalism and would win the annual Carnegie Medal (UK), annual Guardian Prize (UK), and other book awards. The backstory of Adams illustrates the possibilities life has in store if one remains open to what is possible. To remain open, however, one should forgo developing or following some perfect plan. As Jeff Haden wrote in a January 2019 *Inc* article "One of the biggest reasons most people never set out to achieve a huge goal is they think a comprehensively detailed grand plan, one where every step is charted, every milestone identified—where success is pre-ordained, is required."[30] The backstory of Adams becoming an author exemplifies the connection between the embracing ambiguity strategies of allowing one's life to unfold remembering that destiny is a matter of choice.

Assessment: The Brooks Assessment

The following questions are based off David Brooks' observation about the unfolding of life.

- How often do you project how you will feel in the future?
- Why are you doing this?
- Have you ever estimated your future feelings and then, upon reaching that moment realized your feelings are completely different than what you expected?
- Did you even remember those feelings you had about that present moment (what used to be the future) all those days ago?
- Are you so out of touch with reality that you lack the capacity to understand change is a constant?
- Do you catch yourself longing for this consistent feeling?
- Are you afraid that the future will make you feel worse than the present? Why?
- Could the future not be better than the present?
- Does the unknown of the future make you so paralyzed that you are frozen in the present moment?
- Why do you underestimate yourself?
- Why do you lack the capacity to trust your ability to stand upon falling?
- How often in your life have you underestimated yourself?
- Who in your life has made you underestimate yourself?
- Perhaps the question should be "why have you allowed others to underestimate yourself?"
- At your darkest moments why are you spending energy needed for recovery trying to predict the future?
- What good does that do? Instead of thinking about the future, some indeterminate amount of time, why not concentrate on your next step; after all it is the only one you can see in the dark?
- How often do you catch yourself predicting the future when you are stressed?

- Do you understand doing so limits your capacity to grow?
- How often do you make decisions that foreclose future thinking?
- Do you understand that making a decision in the present moment regarding the future has implications that may very well limit your potential?
- Have you thought about your responsibility to your future self?
- Do you acknowledge you have a responsibility to your future self?
- How often do you believe you have control over everything?
- How often do you accept your inability to control your feelings and beliefs?
- Are you so consumed by controlling every aspect of life you forget to live?
- Why must you cling to control so tightly?
- Do you believe that having less control makes you weak? If so, why is that and where does that thinking come from?
- Do you remain humble to your own development?
- Do believe you have more to offer?
- Do you understand that even in your darkest moments you have the potential to unfold, to grow, and to blossom in the future?

Assessment: Three Possible Selves

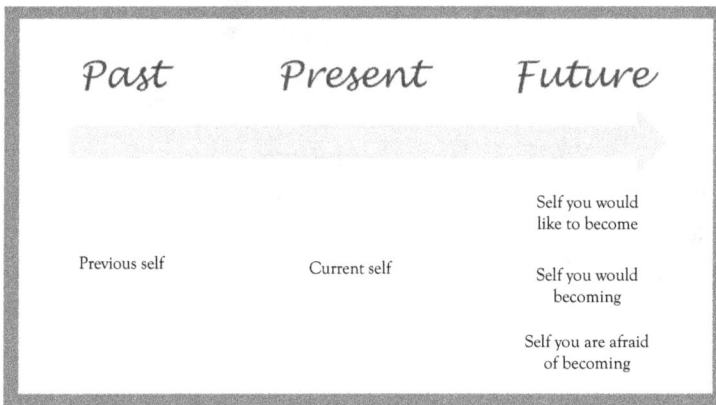

Past	Present	Future
		Self you would like to become
Previous self	Current self	Self you would becoming
		Self you are afraid of becoming

- Are you working toward the ideal self that you would like to become?
- Are you working toward the ideal self that you could become?
- Are you working toward the deal self that you are afraid of becoming?
- How many dreams have you translated into reality?
- How many dreams have you created for yourself?
- Are you dreaming enough so that you always have something to work toward?
- Have you lost touch with people you used to be?
- How often do you think about the person you would like to become, that you could become, and that you are afraid of becoming?

Assessment: Ego Exercise

Directions: To assess your sense of ego, choose between A and B for each of the following pairs. You can use the time-period of last week as a guide. For example, during the last week you thought "me" more than "we."

A	B
Me	We
Separateness	Oneness
Judgment	Compassion
Ignorance	Enlightenment
Hostility	Friendliness
Pride	Humility
Complain	Gratitude
Jealousy	Nonpossessive
Anger	Happiness
Power	Equality
War	Peace
Indifference	Empathy
Fake	Authentic
Busyness	Stillness
Seeking	Knowing

How many B responses did you have? If you have more than 12, you actively cultivated your awakened self; if you had between 6 and 11, you occasionally cultivated an awakened self; and if you had less than 5, you can ask yourself the following question "do I want to set aside my ego and cultivate a more awakened self during the next _____ (pick your time frame)?"

CHAPTER 16

Essential Skill 10: Remind Yourself Destiny Is a Matter of Choice

Reminding yourself destiny is a matter of choice is the 10th essential skill to develop for those interested in embracing the ambiguity of a post-pandemic world. Eighteenth century Venetian author Giacomo Girol-amo Casanova noted "There is no such thing as destiny. We ourselves shape our lives."[1] Two centuries later, American orator and politician William Jennings Bryan made a similar proclamation and wrote "Destiny is not a matter of chance; it is a matter of choice. It is not a thing to be waited for, it is a thing to be achieved."[2] Since the COVID-19 global pandemic, according to Amy Wrzesniewski, "made people think about how they were spending their time, who they were spending it with, and what they spent their time doing," workers across many industries reevaluated their values and realized their destiny was indeed a choice.[3] For example, Allison Lee realized she could create her own destiny and made the choice of quitting her career in digital advertising to work as a stewardess on a 200-foot yacht. While she makes less than she used it, Lee made this choice to create her destiny because "It was a life goal of mine to hit 30 countries before turning 30. But then the pandemic hit. So, now's the time. Not getting any younger. And I did it."[4] To remind yourself, destiny is a matter of choice, history provides evidence of the four strategies included in this section of the training program: make the most of an opportunity, develop your growth mindset, ask yourself how good you want to be, and make sure yesterday does not hold you back from tomorrow.

The first strategy to practice the essential skill of reminding yourself destiny is a matter of choice is to make the most of an opportunity.

Professional baseball player Brian Doyle certainly made the most of his opportunity. This 1978 Major League Baseball (MLB) season was Doyle's sixth as a pro but floundered in the minor leagues. To supplement his minor league income, Doyle held a variety of jobs including selling suits and ties, working as a truck-body builder and officiating football games. During the 1978 MSB season, 23-year-old rookie Doyle was called up and down to the New York Yankees five times. Yankee owner George Steinbrenner wanted to win on the AAA level, so he sent Doyle back down for those playoffs and when the postseason roster expanded to 40 called Doyle back to the Yankees. Three days before the season ended, Willie Randolph, the regular second baseman, pulled a hamstring, so at the end of the season Doyle was playing second. As Doyle recalled "We were in the World Series against the Los Angeles Dodgers. Special permission had to be granted for me to be on the roster because I was not on the regular season roster due to playing in the AAA playoffs. To be granted a roster spot, the Dodgers and MLB Commissioner, Bowie Kuhn, had to approve it. The first game of the World Series was in LA. I was in a cab with Catfish Hunter and Yogi Berra going to the stadium. Yogi looked at me and said, "You're playing kid." I didn't know until just a few hours before the first game of the World Series that I was eligible to play!" And play he did. The 1978 World Series would be the best six games of his professional baseball life. Doyle went seven for 16, drove in two runs, and ended the World Series with a .438 batting average, higher than everyone else, even the Most Valuable Player Bucky Dent.[5]

Doyle's playing career ended in 1981 and after less than four years in the majors, he had a lifetime batting average of .161. He had one brief shining moment in an otherwise mediocre professional baseball career. But no one can take those six games, or his World Series ring, away from him. Doyle made the most of an opportunity. After bouncing around to a few different teams, and even trying his hand in coaching Doyle retired from organized baseball in 1984 and returned to his adopted home of Winter Haven, Florida, to his family of four where he launched a second career in a higher calling. In a 1979 interview he remarked, "there are more important things in life than baseball. One thing is my Christian faith, which is very important to me."[6]

By the 1990s, he had put that faith to work. With just a few college semesters under his belt at Western Kentucky University, and no seminary training, Doyle was ordained as a Southern Baptist minister. He received his first placement in 2005 at the Fort Lauderdale First Baptist Church. Serving there until 2011, Doyle and his wife moved to Georgia where he joined the Global Baseball Youth Federation. First placed by Global Baseball in Israel, Doyle went on to develop the federation's curriculum which took him to Cuba, Puerto Rico, and Ecuador. Brian is the Director of Curriculum and Connie is the Office Administrator of Global Sports Ministry a 501c3 corporation.[7] Brian and Connie have shared over 40 years in professional baseball and over 15 years in ministry. In April 2019, Doyle published his autobiography entitled *The Call: The Desire to Finish Strong.*[8] The book details his life story but the title *The Call*, refers not to getting the call to play MSB, but instead refers to *The Call* of service and ministry to others he received from Jesus. Time and again, Doyle made the most of his opportunities. He had a brief stint in the major leagues but left an indelible mark on Yankee fans everywhere. Once his playing days ended, he made the most of another opportunity and coupled ministry work with baseball. As Scottish-American financial journalist and author Bertie Charles Forbes noted "The man who is intent on making the most of his opportunities is too busy to bother about luck." Doyle was too busy on making the most of his opportunities during the 1978 World Series, and then afterward with his mission work around the world to bother about luck. Doyle understood his destiny was a matter of choice.

Developing a growth mindset is another strategy to practice the essential skill of reminding yourself destiny is a matter of choice. One illustration of a growth mindset comes from the words of Irish playwright George Bernard Shaw who wrote "People are always blaming their circumstances for what they are. I do not believe in circumstances. The people who get on in this world are the people who get up and look for the circumstances that they want, and if they cannot find them, make them." Those with a growth mindset understand they have the opportunity, at any moment, to change their circumstances by learning a new skill, improving their habits, or increasing their knowledge. In short, there is no limit to their growth. While Shaw has a point, it might be more exact to say that "the people who get on in this world" have a growth mindset.

Researchers writing in the Harvard Business Review in an August 2020 article noted such learning and growth opportunities existed during the global pandemic. "While the Covid-19 crisis presents a variety of new challenges, it also creates new opportunities for leaders to cultivate a more expansive growth mindset in themselves and their teams," wrote the authors. Practicing a growth mindset "can help teams to better coordinate, innovate, and own their own futures, making it possible not only to weather the crisis, but to come out of it stronger."[9] Talk of the growth mindset during the pandemic has its origins to the work of Carol Dweck some 15 years earlier.

In her 2006 publication *Mindset: The New Psychology of Success*, Carol Dweck concluded that people have either "fixed" or "growth" mindsets. Some people believe their success is based on innate ability; these are said to have a "fixed" theory of intelligence (fixed mindset). Others, who believe their success is based on hard work, learning, training, and doggedness are said to have a "growth" or an "incremental" theory of intelligence (growth mindset). Dweck's definition of fixed and growth mindsets from a 2012 interview where she said individuals "with a fixed mindset believe their basic abilities, their intelligence, their talents, are just fixed traits. They have a certain amount and that's that, and then their goal becomes to look smart all the time and never look dumb. Those with a growth mindset, however, understand their talents and abilities can be developed through effort, good teaching, and persistence. They don't necessarily think everyone's the same or anyone can be Einstein, but they believe everyone can get smarter if they work at it."[10]

To illustrate the difference between the two mindsets, Dweck uses the example of a student who is struggling at math. The fixed mindset student says: "I'm not good at math. If I don't get A's then I'm a failure. I need to get an A to prove how smart I am." Notice how the fixed mindset student makes a declaratory statement "I am not good at math" declares themselves a failure and has an ego centric reasoning to "get an A to prove how smart they are." The growth mindset student, on the other hand, views things differently and says "I have to work hard to be good at math. If I don't get A's then I need to work harder or try another strategy. I need to get an education in order to be smarter."[11] The growth mindset student takes responsibility for their learning, understands their ability to learn even more than they already do, and stresses the value of education to be smarter. A growth mindset embraces effort, persistence, and assistance when needed as the keys to success. Practicing a growth mindset, and one can indeed practice it, teaches students how challenges and frustration are opportunities for improvement. For example, disruptive, stressful experiences such as the COVID-19 global pandemic, are often opportunities for growth. Researchers publishing in the *Harvard Business Review* noted how crises can help lift the "if it ain't broke, don't fix it" mantra that pervades many organizations, creating new opportunities for people to voice their ideas on how to do things better.[12] After all, asking one's self or others the question "how good do you want to be" is a viable strategy to practice.

A third strategy to practice the essential skill of reminding yourself destiny is a matter of choice is asking yourself how good you want to be. Do you even ask yourself this question? Those that navigate the chaos ask themselves this question quite often as it reminds them of their potential. In his 2008 young adult fantasy novel *The Graveyard Book*, English author Neil Gaiman emphasized the value of recognizing potential when he wrote: "You're alive, Bod. That means you have infinite potential. You can do anything, make anything, dream anything. If you can change the world, the world will change. Potential. Once you're dead, it's gone. Over."[13] Gaiman understood, and then communicated through story, how destiny was a matter of choice for people. But people needed to be reminded of this so Gaiman wrote about three options available to anyone willing to put in the time: potential, dreams, and change. These three options can also help individuals ask the related question of "how good do you want to be?" Maverick British advertising legend Paul Arden recognized his potential and asked himself how good he wanted to be on a daily basis. In fact, in his first book published in 2003, *It's Now How Good You Are, It's How Good You Want To Be*,[14] Arden challenged readers to think about the answer to this question and gave them five choices:

- Pretty good;
- Good;
- Very good;
- The best in your field; or
- The best in the universe.

During the postpandemic VUCA world, asking "how good you want to be?" and then exploring answers to that question, will help individuals and organizations embrace the ambiguity. If such a question is never asked, and therefore never answered, it might be difficult to chart a course forward toward an unknown destination. Arden understood his destination and wanted to be the best advertising mind in the universe. To accomplish this, he thought differently than others. As colleague Dave Trott said of Arden: "Fear of failure, fear of embarrassment, fear of what other people might think, fear of losing our job. All the things that look like insuperable obstacles, Paul just didn't see them; he went right through them as if they weren't there. So, they weren't."[15]

When he was diagnosed with an incurable lung condition, a condition that eventually restricted his movements to the length of the oxygen tube stretching from his breathing machine, Arden directed commercials, wrote advertising campaigns, opened, and ran a photographic gallery, and wrote three best-selling books. When Arden wanted to quit his job as a creative director at one agency to be an art director at Saatchi, it didn't look like a smart move to some people since it was a step down to go from creative director to art director. But he wanted to work at an agency that he admired, with people he admired, so he saw it as a step up. And in his first year at Saatchi, he won a prestigious D&AD award for a brilliant Health Education Council ad highlighting old people dying from hypothermia. He said he wanted to learn to be great at TV ads, not just press ones. "Paul didn't want the predictable, or the expected, the ordinary, or dull, or safe—what was the point? He wanted the risky, the unusual, the daring, which brought with it fear, insecurity and adrenalin. Wasn't that the whole point of being alive?"[16] Paul Arden asked himself "how good he wanted to be" and lived a life answering that question—the best adman in the universe.

Making sure yesterday does not hold you back is another strategy to practice the essential skill of reminding yourself destiny is a matter of choice. Charles F. Kettering was a prominent inventor and the head of research at General Motors for more than 25 years. In 1961, he published a collection of speeches under the title *Prophet of Progress*. One of those speeches stemmed from a luncheon in his honor on the 25th anniversary of his development of the electric self-starter for automobiles where

Kettering noted "I think it is time we turned around and faced the future with our backs to history. You can't have a better tomorrow if you are thinking about yesterday all the time."[17] This relationship, or perhaps dependency, of yesterday, today, and tomorrow, draws an interesting parallel to Newton's Third Law of Motion "for every action (force) in nature there is an equal and opposite reaction. In other words, if object A exerts a force on object B, then object B also exerts an equal and opposite force on object A." Thus, by allowing yesterday (A) to get in the way of today (B), then today (B) will naturally push back against yesterday (A) and have a potentially negative impact on tomorrow (C). This tension between yesterday, today, and tomorrow, will serve as an unnecessary obstacle one needs to hurdle. For example, Amy Owen from Duke University Medical Center found people living with HIV who truly forgave someone who had hurt them in the past, showed positive changes in their immune status. Conversely, remaining in a state of unforgiveness allowed people to hold on to the negative emotions that adversely affect the healing process.[18] Dr. Katherine Piderman, PhD, staff chaplain at the Mayo Clinic in Rochester, Minnesota wrote, "Forgiveness is a decision to let go of resentment and thoughts of revenge. The act that hurt or offended you may always remain a part of your life, but forgiveness can lessen its grip on you and help you focus on other, positive parts of your life."[19]

One person who did not hold on to his yesterday was Shon Hopwood. He was a high school basketball standout, earning himself a scholarship to Midland University in Fremont, Nebraska. After Hopwood realized he was a mediocre talent in basketball, he became disillusioned and did not go to classes. After leaving school, Hopwood joined the U.S. Navy. He was stationed in the Persian Gulf. While in the Navy, Hopwood guarded warships with shoulder-mounted Stinger missiles. He almost died from acute pancreatitis in a Bahrain hospital, which prompted his discharge from the Navy. Hopwood pled guilty on October 28, 1998, to robbing several banks in Nebraska. U.S. District Judge Richard G. Kopf sentenced Hopwood to 12 years, three months in prison followed by three years of supervised release. A *60 Minutes* profile on Hopwood in 2017 told the story of how he discovered he had a brilliant mind for the law when he was serving time for armed bank robbery.[20] He worked in the law library in prison and in an act of self-presentation to see if he could help his own case, Hopwood started studying the law. While he never helped his own case, he did assist other prisoners. Hopwood would go on to be one of the most successful jailhouse lawyers ever—having had one of his cases argued before the U.S. Supreme Court while serving a 12-year sentence for armed bank robbery. Upon being released from prison, he worked full-time while finishing his undergraduate degree. He then got accepted into law school and built a resume as a legal scholar that includes being published in top law journals. He would eventually marry, start a family, and in a tale of redemption as improbable as they come, landed a job teaching at Georgetown University's School of Law. Hopwood could have easily let his yesterday get in the way of his tomorrow. Instead, he moved forward and learned to embrace the ambiguity.[21]

To remind yourself destiny is a matter of choice there are four strategies in this section of the training program: make the most of an opportunity, develop your growth mindset, ask yourself how good you want to be, and make sure yesterday does not hold you back from tomorrow. No matter how severe the issue, the complexity of the problem, or the depth of the low, individuals have the capacity to create their destiny. Aron Lee Ralston, American outdoorsman, mechanical engineer, and motivational speaker is one such example. Ralston is known for surviving an April 2003 canyoneering accident by cutting off his own arm. During a solo descent of Blue John Canyon in southeastern Utah, he dislodged a boulder, pinning his right wrist to the side of the canyon wall. After five days, he was able to amputate his arm with a dull pocketknife, make his way through the rest of the canyon, rappel down a 65-foot (20 m) drop, and hike 7 miles (11 km) to safety. The incident is documented in Ralston's autobiography *Between a Rock and a Hard Place* and is the subject of the 2010 film *127 Hours* where he is portrayed by James Franco. Ralston wrote in his book: "So many people are unhappy and yet will not change their situation. The joy of life comes from new experiences, and there is no greater joy than to have an endlessly changing horizon, for each day to have a new and different sun."[22] Ralston believed destiny was a matter of choice, went to the extreme measure of cutting off his arm, and found his way to safety. Upon learning how to embrace the ambiguity of life with one arm, Ralston went back to mountaineering and became the first person to ascend all of Colorado's fourteeners, defined as a mountain peak with an elevation of at least 14,000 feet, solo in winter. If someone like Ralston can believe he controlled his destiny, surely people in far less extreme situations in the postpandemic environment could do the same.

Assessment: Open-Ended Questions

- How often do you make the most of your opportunities?
- Are you so busy complaining that you are unable to see the opportunities before you?
- Are you so consumed by jealousy that it clouds your ability to even allow yourself the ability to consider an opportunity before you?
- Have you surrendered your fight for self-esteem?
- Have you settled for a life of mediocrity?
- While some people wait for the big leap to appear before them, Botelho and Powell found through their research that the most successful people went looking for one.
- How often do you move forward despite thinking you are not ready?
- How often do you go out and seek a big leap that will challenge you to grow both personally and professionally?

Assessment: Growth Versus Fixed Mindset

Directions: To determine your mindset, select A or B in the following 24 statements:

A: I always want to look smart or talented.   B: I want to learn something new.

A: I never want to fail.   B: I am comfortable with failure.

A: I fear challenges.   B: I embrace challenges.

A: I give up easily.   B: I persist.

A: I blame others.   B: I take responsibility.

A: Giving up is the only option.   B: There must be another way,

A: It is good enough.   B: Is this really my best work?

A: This is too hard.   B: This may take some time and effort

A: I made a mistake.   B: Mistakes help me learn

A: I just cannot do this   B: I am going to train my brain

A: I will never be that smart   B: I will learn how to do this

A: Plan A did not work.   B: There is always a Plan B, or C.

If you selected B statements, nine or more times you have a growth mindset. If you answered B statements, six to eight times you have a mixed mindset. If you selected B, statements five or fewer times you have a fixed mindset. Remember, one mindset is not better than another. Knowing your mindset will, however, help you increase your self-awareness as you continue to navigate the chaos and practice the art of living well.

Exercise: How Good Do You Want to Be?

Directions: This is the shortest assessment in this section. All you have to do is answer one question: "So how good do you want to be?" Only you can answer this question. Take your time. Do some research and figure out if you want to be quite good, the best in the world or somewhere in between. Like most of the assessments included in this training program, your answer to this question will probably change over time.

SO HOW GOOD
DO YOU WANT TO BE?

QUITE GOOD   GOOD   VERY GOOD   THE BEST IN YOUR FIELD   THE BEST IN YOUR WORLD

Assessment: Yesterday Versus Today

Directions: Fortune 500 consultant Christian Muntean has identi-fied six anchors holding people back from moving forward. For each

of the following anchors, ask yourself how often your yesterday of
_____ (fill in one of the anchors) holds you back from today
or tomorrow. For example, how often does fear hold you back from today
or tomorrow? And then explain why it does.

- Fear
- Resentment
- Unforgiveness
- Perfectionism
- Low self-image
- Lack of trust

CHAPTER 17

Conclusion

The COVID-19 pandemic compounded and magnified the forces of volatility, uncertainty, complexity, and ambiguity (VUCA) already reshaping global business and operating models. The ripple effect of this collision between COVID and VUCA will require organizations to continuously innovate, mobilize, and scale new operating models and capabilities this year and in the short term. Much uncertainty remains. According to an EY study published in early 2021, for example, 50 percent of CEOs named uncertainty as the single greatest external threat to the business.[1] What is certain, however, is that "organizations will need to embody agility in all aspects of their enterprise, while adopting a continuous transformation mindset rooted in and motivated by the desire to improve the human experience."[2] Sustaining relevance, vitality, and vibrancy in the postpandemic period will require CEOs to act "boldly and decisively to rewire, retool and reorient their organizations for this new working world. They must tolerate ambiguity, become nimbler, increase their appetite for risk-taking and cultivate agility to pivot quickly toward new opportunities."[3] Embracing ambiguity, however, may be as big a challenge as dealing with uncertainty because, according to an IBM C-Suite study only 41 percent of organizations have the human capital and resources required to execute the necessary and innovate business strategies.[4] To help employees of all levels return to the physical workshop or increase their engagement in the work itself, organizations looking to embrace the ambiguity of the postpandemic VUCA world would serve themselves well by reminding people of their unlimited potential if given the chance.

American author Augustine "Og" Mandino provides a case study in someone who needed to be reminded of his potential. Mandino sold over 50 million books and had his works translated into over 25 languages. His path to success, however, much like so many others, was long and uncertain. In his 1975 *The Greatest Miracle in World* Mandino proclaimed that most people "in varying degrees, are already dead. In one way or another they have lost their dreams, their ambitions, their desire for a better life." This echoes the observation of other authors through the ages like Henry David Thoreau. In his 1854 essay entitled "Walden," Thoreau wrote that "most men lead lives of quiet desperation." Mandino went further, however, and suggested that most people rise the level of mediocrity, surrender their fight for self-esteem, and compromise their great potential. Such an approach meant that people were "no more than living deaths confined to cemeteries of their choice." There is another way to live, however, as people "need not remain in that state. They can be resurrected from their sorry condition. They can each perform the greatest miracle in the world. They can each come back from the dead."[5] That's exactly what Mandino did. He came back from contemplating suicide, choose forward action instead of inertia, and become one of the most influential self-help authors of the 20th century.

Rising from the depths of despair like Mandino, however, requires courage, grit, and a commitment to change. Changing the direction of one's life requires an extraordinary physical, mental, and emotional energy. Even after a year of a global pandemic, however, most people remain hesitant to live the life they have envisioned. Yes, as discussed earlier, some people did indeed leverage the reflection time afforded them during the lockdown and discover a new path to travel in life. Those individuals formed a small minority. As David Brooks reminded readers in a May 27, 2021, *New York Times* column "we have more to fear from our inhibitions than from our vulnerabilities. More lives are wrecked by the slow and frigid death of emotional closedness than by the short and hot risks of emotional openness."[6] Quitting a job, changing careers, starting a business, going back to school, and the myriad of other decisions available to those willing to ask themselves challenges one to overcome what behavioral economists call the status quo bias.[7] The status quo bias is a cognitive bias where people remain predisposed to hold on to their current circumstances, however difficult they may be, instead of taking a risk and altering the course of their life in a new direction. There is growing evidence that the pandemic will abate sooner rather than later, and the economy will rebound. "But even when life improves, it's useful to remember that the status quo is often not as steady and reliable as it seems."[8]

Back in 2008, in the midst of another historic event, often referred to as the Great Recession, the writer Sady Doyle offered up her own reflections on the false allure of the status quo. She discussed the comfort associated with the status quo bias. It is far easier to remain in their comfort zone. Such a life approach is wrong Doyle argued, and reminded readers about life's ambiguity when she wrote: "You are never safe. Loss and change are constants. You will never be safe, and you may not always be happy—but you owe it to yourself to start asking the question—how will I change my life?"[9] Some individuals took advantage of their isolation during the pandemic to ask that question. Will more follow suit in the postpandemic period? That remains to be seen. But for those willing to embrace ambiguity, remember the comfort zone of mediocrity the status quo provides as it may just be the catalyst needed to recognize the allure of inertia, ask such an important question, and explore answers outside of one's comfort zone.

Commenting on the postpandemic marketplace, Tracy Brower observed "amid ambiguity, an unquenchable curiosity will rule the day. Openness and desire to learn are good, but you will need a craving to learn, understand and know more about a wider variety of things."[10] Justin Small echoed similar sentiment in an April 2021 article when he noted "Managing uncertainty in the workplace is essential for today's leaders and can be the difference between a business's success or demise. Adaptability, agility, and courage are the powerful tools needed for business leaders to effectively manage the unknown" in order to embrace the ambiguity of the postpandemic marketplace and pull through such challenging times.[11] Moreover, in a December 2020, *Forbes* article Ulrik Juul Christensen succinctly noted "companies must forge and shape the competency of their workforce—deliberately, purposefully, and strategically."[12]

One company embracing ambiguity and shaping the competency of their workforce is General Motors (GM). In April 2021, GM launched it "work appropriately" strategy as its surprisingly simple return to work approach post pandemic. CEO Mary Barra and other GM leaders announced the flexible, evolving policy that will differ depending on the employee, week and project and demonstrates the organization's commitment to embracing ambiguity. As Laura Jones, GM's global talent director said, "This is an evolution of our culture for everyone, and it is not about a policy or a one-size-fits-all approach."[13] GM's postpandemic work approach employs the same simplistic, yet ambiguous strategy Barra used to reduce the 10-page dress code policy with two words "dress appropriately" when she was leading human resources from 2009 to 2011. As Michael Wayland summarized "such flexible and ambiguous policies are meant to empower GM's leaders to take responsibility for their departments and employees."[14]

The Essential Skills provide a toolkit for anyone with a "craving to learn, understand and know more about a wider variety of things." While the longing for a prepandemic "normal" will continue in the near future, accepting the existence and permanence of chaos (Essential Skill 1) will provide a much-needed perspective of reality. Such a vantage point can then propel one to challenge their assumptions and think differently (Essential Skill 2). A craving to learn and consider different viewpoints will help one connect and empower others (Essential Skill 3) in the postpandemic world. But supporting others requires one demonstrate a strong work ethic (Essential Skill 4) while simultaneously experimenting with life (Essential Skill 5). Embracing the ambiguity of the postpandemic world leverages such experimentation while reminding people to travel outside their comfort zone (Essential Skill 6). With managing the stress and anxiety (Essential Skill 7) of being uncomfortable and embracing ambiguity, individuals will serve themselves well by understanding the role of nuance in their decision-making process (Essential Skill 8) as they remain open to the unfolding of life (Essential Skill 9). Just as Mandino reminded readers decades ago that they have the power to rise from the inertia of the status quo (or what he labeled "rise from the dead"), those who wish to embrace the ambiguity of the postpandemic world should remind themselves destiny is a matter of choice (Essential Skill 10).

Will you be ready? Will you engage in the reflection, self-awareness, and time required to assess how often you practice each of the Essential Skills? Will you be able to embrace the ambiguity of the postpandemic VUCA environment? Will your organization? Will your organization's leadership recognize the need to embrace the ambiguity of the postpandemic world? My hope is that this publication and Essential Skills training program provides some small degree of support for those who are interested in embracing ambiguity and thriving in the postpandemic world of tomorrow.

Notes

Preface

1. White (November 01, 2017).
2. Keynes (1936).
3. Global Risks Report (2021).
4. Allen (April 07, 2021).
5. Unemployment Rates, OECD (April 12, 2021).
6. Berman (April 01, 2021).
7. Shaping the Trends of Our Times (September 2020).
8. Chan (April 21, 2021).
9. MacCarthy and Propp (May 04, 2021).
10. Cave et al. (May 22, 20121).
11. Huxley (July 22, 2008).
12. Houle (October 11, 2020).
13. Stearns (1998).
14. Roush (May 11, 2021).
15. Roush (May 11, 2021).
16. Dale Chihuly Biography.

Chapter 1

1. Kochhar (March 18, 2021).
2. World Health Organization (February 28, 2021).
3. World Health Organization (February 28, 2021).
4. World Health Organization (February 28, 2021).
5. COVID-19 Dashboard by the Center for Systems Science and Engineering (CSSE) (February 28, 2021).
6. World Economic Forum (2021).
7. Impact of the coronavirus pandemic on the global economy—Statistics & Facts, published by Statista Research Department, February 23, 2021.
8. Jones et al. (January 24, 2021).
9. McKinsey Global Institute (February 18, 2021).
10. Crutsinger (October 13, 2020).
11. International Monetary Fund (IMF) (October 2020).
12. Kochhar (March 18, 2021).
13. Agility: The antidote to complexity (April 2021).

14. Walmsley et al. (December 10, 2020).
15. Walmsley et al. (December 10, 2020).
16. Gould (March 05, 2021).
17. Gould (March 05, 2021).
18. Kurtz (January 08, 2021).
19. Kurtz (January 08, 2021).
20. Pilon (December 08, 2020).
21. Tiefenbacher (December 31, 2019).
22. Cowen (January 13, 2021).
23. Govaert and Cao (July 22, 2020).
24. Boehnert (November 2018).
25. Bryant (August 05, 2020).
26. Deaton (2018); Gilman (2017) and Fuchs et al. (2020).
27. Global Internet Penetration (March 01, 2021).
28. Global Internet Penetration (March 01, 2021).
29. Ali (September 15, 2020).
30. Ali (September 15, 2020).
31. Latest Technology Trends That Will Impact Businesses in 2021 (May 20, 2021).
32. The social enterprise in a world disrupted: Leading the shift from survive to thrive (2021).

Chapter 2

1. Worley, and Jules (June 16, 2020).
2. Garton and Mankins (December 01, 2020).
3. Garton and Mankins (December 01, 2020).
4. Casey, Jr (n.d.).
5. McChrystal and Fussell (March 23, 2020).
6. Busteed (February 25, 2014).
7. Busteed (February 25, 2014).
8. McChrystal and Fussell (March 23, 2020).
9. The Work of the Future: Building Better Jobs in an Age of Intelligent Machines (2020).
10. Kropp (January 14, 2021).
11. Luhby and Tappe (February 02, 2021).
12. Kane et al. (February 10, 2021).
13. The Future of Work: Workplace Trends for 2021 and Beyond (February 22, 2021).
14. The Future of Work: Workplace Trends for 2021 and Beyond (February 22, 2021).

15. Gobrin (February 23, 2021).
16. Moving beyond remote: Workplace transformation in the wake of COVID-19 (October 07, 2020).
17. The future of work after COVID-19 (February 18, 2021).
18. Goldberg (January 28, 2021).
19. Gobrin (May 06, 2020).
20. Gobrin (February 23, 2021)
21. Living in a VUCA world: How modern leaders are evolving to navigate disruption (February 24, 2020).
22. Cranston (November 15, 2020).
23. Cranston (November 15, 2020).
24. Emerging From a "VUCA" World - How Sales Leaders Can Set a Course for Less Stress in 2021 (January 25, 2021).
25. IBM (2021).
26. IBM (2021).
27. Kane et al. (February 10, 2021).
28. Agility: The antidote to complexity (April 2021).
29. Agility: The antidote to complexity (April 2021).
30. Rigby et al. (May 15, 2020).
31. Rigby et al. (May 15, 2020).
32. Emrich (December 17, 2020).
33. Borges (August 26, 2019).
34. Ninth International Forum on Project Management: In the Pandemic's New Normal, Enterprises Need to Go Beyond Agility (April 26, 2021).
35. Melnyk (May 05, 2021).
36. Hyder (May 04, 2021).
37. Jones (February 22, 2021).
38. Sayed (April 27, 2021).
39. The Conference Board (April 2021).
40. Ninth International Forum on Project Management: In the Pandemic's New Normal, Enterprises Need to Go Beyond Agility (April 26, 2021).

Chapter 3

1. King (September 13, 2012).
2. Bernhard (June 26, 2014).
3. Seneca, *Moral Letters to Lucilius*, "Letter XVIII: On Festivals and Fasting," 65 AD, https://sites.google.com/site/thestoiclife/the_teachers/seneca/letters/018
4. Seneca, *Moral Letters to Lucilius*, "Letter XVIII: On Festivals and Fasting," 65 AD, https://sites.google.com/site/thestoiclife/the_teachers/seneca/letters/018

5. An Intellectual Entente (September 10, 2009).
6. An Intellectual Entente (September 10, 2009).
7. Haynie (April 27, 2021).
8. Samuel (June 09, 2020).
9. Samuel (June 09, 2020).
10. Roose (April 21, 2021).
11. Levitz (April 11, 2021).
12. Levitz (April 11, 2021).
13. Long (May 07, 2021).
14. Kochhar (March 18, 2021).
15. Long (May 07, 2021).
16. Roose (April 21, 2021).
17. Is This Working?: Pulse of the American Worker Survey: Special Report (March 2021).
18. Isay (May 13, 2020).
19. Díaz and Turits.
20. Weldon (August 30, 2020).
21. Díaz and Turits (n.d.).
22. In Pandemic Era's Isolation, Meaning of 'Self-Care' Evolves (November 24, 2020).
23. Clay (July 01, 2020).
24. Barth (May 13, 2019).
25. Schwarz (n.d.).
26. Neff (February 17, 2016).
27. McEvers (May 10, 2017).
28. Twenge (2014).
29. The American Freshman: National Norms.
30. Wikipedia entry (March 12, 2021).
31. Congressional Research Service (January 13, 2021).
32. Smialek (May 14, 2020).
33. Damme (n.d.)
34. Lazear (August 04, 2020).

Chapter 4

1. Kail (August 19, 2013).
2. Kail (August 19, 2013).
3. Arbesman (2016).
4. Is Microsoft Office Proficiency Still Needed Nowadays? (January 12, 2021).

5. Soft Skills vs. Hard Skills in the Workplace (n.d).
6. Lau (January 20, 2021).
7. Anderson (January 09, 2020).
8. Flanagan and Gregory (2019).
9. Kolakowski (September 10, 2019).
10. Wiles (October 23, 2020).
11. World Economic Forum (October 2020).
12. Burning Glass Technologies (February 2021).
13. Alliance (n.d.).
14. Look for skills, not credentials': Beth Cobert on tapping into US talent (February 26, 2021).
15. Amour (December 17, 2020).
16. Cacciattolo (May 2015).
17. Friedman (October 20, 2020).
18. Look for skills, not credentials: Beth Cobert on tapping into US talent (February 26, 2021).
19. Wiles (October 23, 2020).
20. Haynie (April 27, 2021).
21. Skills for 2030: Conceptual learning framework
22. Skills for 2030: Conceptual learning framework (2019).
23. Moran (October 27, 2020).
24. Moran (October 27, 2020).
25. Knowles (1975).
26. Gutierrez (May 24, 2017).
27. Lombardozzi (2020).
28. Bakhshi et al. (2017).
29. Friedman (October 20, 2020).
30. Friedman (October 20, 2020).
31. Khan (July 06, 2020).
32. Upston (September 28, 2020).
33. 2019 Deloitte Global Human Capital Trends (2019).
34. Dillon (August 15, 2017).
35. Friedman (October 20, 2020).
36. Emily He (September 22, 2020).

Chapter 5

1. Wiles (May 22, 2020).
2. Brower (February 14, 2021).
3. Wiles (May 22, 2020).

4. Lieberman (March 02, 2021).

5. Bernhard (November 07, 2019).

6. Davis and Hayes (July/August 2012).

7. Miller (December 19, 2019).

8. Miller (December 19, 2019).

9. Nichols et al. (April 02, 2020).

10. Lieberman (March 02, 2021).

11. Wyer (January 23, 2013); Horn and Moesta (January 06, 2020).

12. Berr (May 17, 2016).

13. Wilkie (October 21, 2019).

14. Stolzenberg et al. (2020).

15. Ruddock and Craig (April 23, 2021).

16. Jezard (June 01, 2018).

17. The OECD Future of Education and Skills 2030: Conceptual Learning Framework (2019).

18. Workforce of the future: The competing forces shaping 2030 (2019).

19. Jain (April 28, 2021).

20. Jain (April 28, 2021).

21. Martin (2012).

22. Goldberg (January 28, 2021).

23. Vajda (March 04, 2016).

24. Coronavirus: How can society thrive post-pandemic? (November 18, 2020).

25. Pir (January 20, 2021).

26. Herrera (February 06, 2021).

27. Herrera (December 01, 2019).

28. Herrera (December 01, 2019).

29. Herrera (February 06, 2021).

Chapter 6

1. Huxley (1958).

2. Colagrossi (June 03, 2019).

3. Pichai (March 11, 2021).

4. Rainie and Anderson (May 03, 2017).

5. Moon (June 03, 2020).

6. Botelho and Powell (2017).

7. Cohan (January 29, 2021).

8. DeSimone and Robison (January 23, 2021).

9. Schawbel (August 04, 2015).

10. *Data Driven: What Students Need to Succeed in A Rapidly Changing Business World* (February 2015).

Chapter 7

1. Carr (July/August 2008).
2. Hepps (July 24, 2014).
3. Kinney (January 18, 2021).
4. Kinney (January 18, 2021).
5. Rosenthal (May 19, 2019).
6. Guse (January 30, 2020).
7. Guse (January 30, 2020).
8. Fitzsimmons (December 02, 2018).
9. Kinney (January 18, 2021).
10. Pace (February 11, 1992).
11. Pace (February 11, 1992).
12. Pace (February 11, 1992).
13. www.goodreads.com/book/show/3521748-letters-1
14. Fox (December 19, 2015).
15. Tsioulcas (December 19, 2015).
16. Fox (December 19, 2015).
17. Fox (December 19, 2015).
18. Smith (February 22, 2020).
19. Pryor and Bright (2012).
20. Pryor and Bright (2012).
21. Warrell (July 15, 2015).
22. Warrell (July 15, 2015).
23. Miglani (2013).

Chapter 8

1. Bartmann (n.d.).
2. Gaskell (May 11, 2020).
3. Harrington and Ruppel (December 1999).
4. Parker (July 30, 2020).
5. Petrow (October 08, 2020).
6. Petrow (October 08, 2020).
7. Carmen (May 15, 2020).
8. Carmen (May 15, 2020).
9. Carmen (May 15, 2020).
10. Cadsby (July 25, 2011).
11. Cadsby (July 25, 2011).
12. Tetlock (2006).
13. Menand (November 27, 2005).

14. Kahneman (2011).
15. Schrage (Winter 2003).
16. Tay (June 01, 2020).
17. Kahneman (2011)
18. Association of American Colleges & Universities (Spring 2013).
19. Talbert (November 04, 2010).
20. Talbert (November 04, 2010).
21. Duckworth et al. (2007).
22. Edelman (1993).
23. Edelman (1993).
24. Howkins (2013).
25. Hennessy (January/February 2002).
26. Herrera and Carlson (n.d.).
27. Ludden (November 16, 2016).
28. Project Implicit website (n.d.).
29. Project Implicit website (n.d.).
30. Malcolm Gladwell, Blink: The Power of Thinking Without Thinking (2005).
31. James (September 01, 2006).
32. James (September 01, 2006).
33. Brooks (May 27, 2021).
34. Brooks (May 27, 2021).

Chapter 9

1. Zoom sees more growth after 'unprecedented' 2020 (March 01, 2021).
2. Anderson et al. (February 18, 2021).
3. Hirsch (July 10, 2020).
4. Hirsch (July 10, 2020).
5. Nussbaum (June 01, 2003).
6. Tutu (2000).
7. Remarks by President Obama at Memorial Service for Former South African President
8. Hartley (October 21, 2020).
9. Matt Murray made a heartwarming gesture to Jacob Markstrom after his father passed away (n.d.).
10. Seppälä and Cameron (December 01, 2015).
11. McKinsey (May 01, 2020).
12. Hougaard et al. (December 04, 2020).
13. Hougaard et al. (December 04, 2020).
14. Perry (2007).

15. Yates (January 14, 2021).
16. Greenway (April 26, 2018).
17. Christensen (May 15, 2012).
18. Mental Health, Substance Use, and Suicidal Ideation During the COVID-19 Pandemic—United States, June 24–30, 2020." (August 14, 2020).
19. Panchal et al. (February 10, 2021).
20. Estes (March 29, 2021).
21. Estes (March 29, 2021).

Chapter 10

1. Bernd (n.d.).
2. Lillard (December 12, 2020).
3. Dienstbier (1989).
4. Goggins (March 19, 2018).
5. Goggins (November 11, 2017).
6. Goggins (November 11, 2017).
7. Maxwell (January 14, 2015).
8. Parker (n.d.).
9. Guengerich (October 16, 2015).
10. Daily Plain Dealer (January 15, 1859).
11. Gross (May 12, 2021).
12. The Making of Full Metal Jacket (July 16, 2014).
13. Full Metal Jacket Interview (June 21, 2017).
14. The Making of Full Metal Jacket (July 16, 2014).
15. Adams (2013).
16. Roush (May 11, 2021).
17. Roush (May 11, 2021).

Chapter 11

1. www.goodreads.com/quotes/14033-question-i-am-interested-in-so-many-things-and-i
2. Bregman (April 28, 2010).
3. Boyes (November 09, 2018).
4. Schuessler (October 11, 2017).
5. Chief of Chobani (April 09, 2017).
6. Chief of Chobani (April 09, 2017).
7. Farina (n.d.).
8. Popova (n.d.).
9. Citizenship in a Republic (May 02, 2021).

10. Citizenship in a Republic (May 02, 2021).
11. History of the Peloponnesian War, translated from the Greek of Thucydides. (1836).
12. Airman 1st Class William H. Pitsenbarger (May 18, 2015).
13. Airman 1st Class William H. Pitsenbarger (May 18, 2015).
14. Bailey (January 25, 2017).
15. MIller (December 27, 2016).
16. Mirren (n.d.).
17. Diamond (November 28, 2017).
18. Richards (September 25, 2017).
19. Rich (August 20, 2012).

Chapter 12

1. Parrott (September 10, 2020).
2. Vidal (January 27, 2016).
3. Bannister's Four-Minute Mile Named Greatest Athletic Achievement (November 18, 2005).
4. Mile run world record progression.
5. Bannister's Four-Minute Mile Named Greatest Athletic Achievement (November 18, 2005).
6. Huber (June 09, 2017).
7. Pappas (2021).
8. Huston (January 02, 2021).
9. Parker-Pope (July 07, 2016).
10. Martel (2002).
11. Martel (2002).
12. Flood (July 22, 2014).
13. Blume (n.d.).
14. Blume (2014).
15. Eggersten (June 19, 2015).
16. Dargis (May 15, 2016).
17. Dargis (May 15, 2016).
18. Belluldi (August 28, 2016).
19. Synnott (October 03, 2018).
20. How I Climbed a 3,000-Foot Vertical Cliff—Without Ropes: Alex Honnold (March 16, 2019).
21. Martin (May 24, 2019).
22. Honnold and Roberts (2015).
23. Kaufman (September 29, 2010).

Chapter 13

1. Nicholson (February 18, 2021).
2. Bunch (March 15, 2021).
3. Bunch (March 15, 2021).
4. Gardner (2009).
5. Gigerenzer (2004).
6. Gigerenzer (2004).
7. Church (December 18, 2020).
8. Church (December 18, 2020).
9. Brooks (2014).
10. Shallcross et al. (n.d.).
11. Brooks (2014).
12. Hammond (March 18, 2014).
13. The Story Behind the Iconic 'Kiss of Life' Photo (April 17, 2017).
14. The Story Behind the Iconic 'Kiss of Life' Photo (April 17, 2017).
15. 36 Years Later, NC Man Thanks Red Sox Star For Saving Life (August 08, 2018).
16. 36 Years Later, NC Man Thanks Red Sox Star For Saving Life (August 08, 2018).
17. Hughes (October 16, 2018).
18. Newman (November 19, 2016).
19. Fagerholm (July 29, 2016).
20. 2021 Emerging From the Pandemic Survey (February 24, 2021).
21. History Quotes (n.d.).

Chapter 14

1. Adams (2013).
2. Collins (June 18, 2018).
3. Adams (2013).
4. Eisenhower's Urgent/Important Principle (n.d.).
5. Eisenhower's Urgent/Important Principle (n.d.).
6. Schwartzberg (April 27, 2021).
7. Schwartzberg (April 27, 2021).
8. Marczi (May 27, 2020).
9. Tolle (2004).
10. Liu (April 19, 2021).
11. Becker (n.d.).
12. Coelho (May 10, 2017).

13. Jantz (January 03, 2017).
14. Covey (1989).
15. Berger (July 17, 2001).
16. Graham (May 21, 2021).
17. Koehn (April 03, 2020).

Chapter 15

1. Carucci (March 30, 2020).
2. Carucci (March 30, 2020).
3. Brooks (April 02, 2012).
4. Brooks (April 02, 2012).
5. Batchelor (1998).
6. Batchelor (1998).
7. Batchelor (1998).
8. Hazel and Paula (1986).
9. Slouching Towards Bethlehem.
10. Carroll (1865).
11. Cohen (October 2014).
12. Anderton (March 16, 2020).
13. Anderton (March 16, 2020).
14. Kenny (July 8, 2020).
15. Tolle (2005).
16. Tolle (2005).
17. Pauley (May 12, 2019).
18. Seelye (January 07, 2021).
19. www.goodreads.com/quotes/61242-i-pay-no-attention-whatever-to-any-body-s-praise-or-blame
20. 10 Things You Might Not Know About ROCKY (December 26, 2019).
21. Brown (2017).
22. Brown (2017).
23. 20 Quotes for Letting Go of the Past and Moving on With Your Life (August 26, 2017).
24. Schwartz (n.d.).
25. Schwartz (n.d.).
26. Michel de Montaigne (n.d.).
27. Leigh (November 24, 2016).
28. Roger Federer: Never Stop Improving, Goalcoast (April 03, 2017).
29. Flood (January 04, 2015).
30. Haden (January 02, 2018).

Chapter 16

1. Cave et al. (May 22, 20121).
2. William Jennings Bryan quotes (n.d.).
3. Schwab (May 04, 2021).
4. Schwab (May 04, 2021).
5. Madison (Summer 2015).
6. Madison (Summer 2015).
7. Global Sports Website.
8. Doyle (2019).
9. Ashford et al. (August 20, 2020).
10. https://sbctc.instructure.com/courses/1934284/pages/3-dot-4-a-receptive-mindset?module_item_id=41213570
11. https://sbctc.instructure.com/courses/1934284/pages/3-dot-4-a-receptive-mindset
12. Ashford et al. (August 20, 2020).
13. Gaiman (2008).
14. Arden (2003).
15. Trott (April 09, 2008).
16. Arden (April 09, 2008).
17. Prophet of Progress
18. Schiano (August 06, 2018).
19. Schiano (August 06, 2018).
20. From bank robber to law professor (October 12, 2017).
21. From bank robber to law professor (October 12, 2017).
22. Ralston (2005).

Chapter 17

1. What unseen megatrends will shape your transformation?
2. Bruce (January 07, 2020).
3. Bruce (January 07, 2020).
4. The enterprise guide to closing the skills gap.
5. Mandino (1975).
6. Brooks (May 27, 2021).
7. Status quo bias.
8. Todd (May 21, 2021).
9. Todd (May 21, 2021).
10. Brower (February 14, 2021).
11. Small (April 03, 2021).

12. Christensen (December 29, 2020).
13. Wayland (April 20, 2021).
14. Wayland (April 20, 2021).

References

"10 Things You Might Not Know About ROCKY." December 26, 2019. www.warpedfactor.com/2014/12/10-things-you-might-not-know-about-rocky.html?m=1

"20 Quotes for Letting Go of the Past and Moving on With Your Life." August 26, 2017. www.huffpost.com/entry/20-quotes-for-letting-go-_b_11698272

"36 Years Later, NC Man Thanks Red Sox Star for Saving Life." *WNCN*, August 08, 2018. www.wfmynews2.com/article/news/local/36-years-later-nc-man-thanks-red-sox-star-for-saving-life/83-581599283

2021 Emerging From the Pandemic Survey, February 24, 2021. www.willistowerswatson.com/en-US/Insights/2021/02/2021-emerging-from-the-pandemic-survey

Adams, S. 2013. "How to Fail at Almost Everything and Still Win Big: Kind of the Story of My Life." www.amazon.com/How-Fail-Almost-Everything-Still/dp/1591846919/ref=tmm_hrd_swatch_0?_encoding=UTF8&qid=&sr=

"Airman 1st Class William H. Pitsenbarger." May 18, 2015. www.nationalmuseum.af.mil/Visit/Museum-Exhibits/Fact-Sheets/Display/Article/195918/airman-1st-class-william-h-pitsenbarger/

"Aldous Huxley." *The Guardian*, July 22, 2008. www.theguardian.com/books/2008/jun/13/aldous.huxley

Ali, A. September 15, 2020. "Here's What Happens Every Minute on the Internet in 2020." *Visual Capitalist*, www.visualcapitalist.com/every-minute-internet-2020/

Allen, T. April 07, 2021. "The Pandemic Is Changing Employee Benefits." *Harvard Business Review*, https://hbr.org/2021/04/the-pandemic-is-changing-employee-benefits

"An Intellectual Entente." *Harvard Magazine*, September 10, 2009. https://harvardmagazine.com/breaking-news/james-watson-edward-o-wilson-intellectual-entente

Anderson, B. January 09, 2020. "The Most In-Demand Hard and Soft Skills of 2020." *LinkedIn*, https://business.linkedin.com/talent-solutions/blog/trends-and-research/2020/most-in-demand-hard-and-soft-skills

Anderson, J., L. Rainie, and E.A. Vogels. February 18, 2021. "Emerging Change." *Pew Research Center*, www.pewresearch.org/internet/2021/02/18/emerging-change/

Anderton, J. March 16, 2020. "Daniel Radcliffe Says End of 'Harry Potter' Contributed to His Alcohol Abuse." *Yahoo News*, https://news.yahoo.com/daniel-radcliffe-says-end-harry-163700737.html

Arbesman, S. 2016. "Overcomplicated: Technology at the Limits of Comprehension." www.amazon.com/gp/product/1591847761/ref=as_li_ss_tl?&linkCode=sl1&tag=digitont-20&linkId=8a74ac533d2cf6972a9ba709d7f918b3

Arden, P. 2003. "It's Not How Good You Are, It's How Good You Want to Be: The World's Bestselling Book by Paul Arden." https://tinyurl.com/nftd3u56

Ashford, S.J., M. Sytch, and L.L. Greer. August 20, 2020. "5 Ways a Crisis Can Help You Cultivate a Growth Mindset." *Harvard Business Review*, https://hbr.org/2020/08/5-ways-a-crisis-can-help-you-cultivate-a-growth-mindset

Association of American Colleges & Universities. Spring 2013. "It Takes More Than a Major: Employer Priorities for College Learning and Student Success." www.aacu.org/publications-research/periodicals/it-takes-more-major-employer-priorities-college-learning-and

Bailey, C. January 25, 2017. "Stay Afriad, but Do It Anyway." www.nbacares.org/stories-and-news/stay-afraid

Bakhshi, H., J.M. Downing, M.A. Osborne, and P. Schneider. 2017. "The Future of Skills Employment in 2030." *Pearson,* https://futureskills.pearson.com/research/assets/pdfs/technical-report.pdf

"Bannister's Four-Minute Mile Named Greatest Athletic Achievement." *Forbes,* November 18, 2005. www.forbes.com/2005/11/18/bannister-four-minute-mile_cx_de_lr_1118bannister.html?sh=66ba0e0d2e8f

Barth, F.D. May 13, 2019. "Self-Care Is Important: Why Is It So Hard to Practice?" *Psychology Today,* www.psychologytoday.com/us/blog/the-couch/201905/self-care-is-important-why-is-it-so-hard-practice

Bartmann, N. n.d. "Senior Behavioral Researcher, Center for Advanced Hindsight at Duke University." www.sbm.org/behavioral-medicine-during-the-time-of-covid-19/separating-work-life-from-home-life-during-covid-19

Batchelor, S. 1998. "Buddhism Without Beliefs: A Contemporary Guide to Awakening." www.amazon.com/Buddhism-Without-Beliefs-Contemporary-Awakening/dp/1573226564

Becker, L. n.d. www.drbecker-phelps.com/home/

Belluldi, N. August 28, 2016. "Inspirational Quotations by Johann Wolfgang von Goethe (#647)." *Right Attitudes,* www.rightattitudes.com/2016/08/28/johann-wolfgang-von-goethe/

Berger, M. July 17, 2001. "Katharine Graham, Former Publisher of Washington Post, Dies at 84." *The New York Times,* www.nytimes.com/2001/07/17/obituaries/katharine-graham-former-publisher-of-washington-post-dies-at-84.html

Berman, J. April 01, 2021. "A Reckoning in Bubble Assets is Coming." *Forbes,* www.forbes.com/sites/jamesberman/2021/04/01/a-reckoning-in-bubble-assets-is-coming/?sh=196b7867677e

Bernd, K. n.d. "10 Incredible Quotes From The U.S. Women's Soccer Team." *Athlete Network*, https://an.athletenetwork.com/blog/10-quotes-us-womens-soccer-team

Bernhard, T. June 26, 2014. "Surprisingly Modern Wisdom from Ancient Greeks and Romans." *Psychology Today*, www.psychologytoday.com/us/blog/turning-straw-gold/201406/surprisingly-modern-wisdom-ancient-greeks-and-romans

Bernhard, T. November 07, 2019. "Equanimity: The Key to Happiness." *Psychology Today*, www.psychologytoday.com/us/blog/turning-straw-gold/201911/equanimity-the-key-happiness

Berr, J. May 17, 2016. "Employers: New College Grads Aren't Ready for Workplace." *CBS News*, www.cbsnews.com/news/employers-new-college-grads-arent-ready-for-workplace/

Blume, J. 2014. "Tiger Eyes." www.amazon.com/Tiger-Eyes-Judy-Blume/dp/1481413872/ref=sr_1_1?dchild=1&keywords=tiger+eyes+blume&qid=1621084763&sr=8-1

Blume, J. n.d. "A Biography." www.google.com/books/edition/Judy_Blume/FhM0s7SzecoC?hl=en&gbpv=1&dq=judy+blume+biography&printsec=frontcover

Boehnert, J. November 2018. "The Visual Representation of Complexity: Definitions, Examples, and Learning Points." https://tinyurl.com/2xee9fbr

Borges, H. August 26, 2019. "Leading in Complex Times, from VUCA to Complexity." https://helio-borges.medium.com/https-medium-com-hborgesg-leading-in-complex-times-6b583acf955

Botelho, E., and K. Powell. 2017. "The CEO Next Door: The 4 Behaviors that Transform Ordinary People into World-Class Leaders." *Penguin*.

Boyes, A. November 09, 2018. "50 Ideas for Five Day Self-Experiments." *Psychology Today*, www.psychologytoday.com/us/blog/in-practice/201811/50-ideas-five-day-self-experiments

Bregman, P. April 28, 2010. "Why Not Having a Plan Can Be the Best Plan of All." *Harvard Business Review*, https://hbr.org/2010/04/how-to-make-a-career-when-you.html

Brooks, A.W. 2014. "Get Excited Reappraising Pre-Performance Anxiety as Excitement." *Journal of Experimental Psychology*, www.apa.org/pubs/journals/releases/xge-a0035325.pdf

Brooks, D. April 02, 2012. "Respect the Future." *New York Times*, www.nytimes.com/2012/04/03/opinion/brooks-respect-the-future.html

Brooks, D. May 27, 2021. "The Great Unmasking." *The New York Times*, www.nytimes.com/2021/05/27/opinion/coronavirus-masks-vaccine.html?action=click&module=Opinion&pgtype=Homepage

Brower, T. February 14, 2021. "The Future of Work Will Demand These 8 New Skills." *Forbes*, www.forbes.com/sites/tracybrower/2021/02/14/the-future-of-work-will-demand-these-8-new-skills/?sh=3eb9893822e6

Brown, B. 2017. "Rising Strong: How the Ability to Reset Transforms the Way We Live, Love, Parent, and Lead." www.amazon.com/Rising-Strong-Ability-Transforms-Parent/dp/081298580X/ref=sr_1_3?dchild=1&keywords=Rising+Strong%3A+How+the+Ability+to+Reset+Transforms+the+Way+We+Live%2C+Love%2C+Parent%2C+and+Lead&qid=1621693465&sr=8-3

Bruce, J. January 07, 2020. "The Future of Work Is Now: Embrace The Uncertainty." *Forbes,* www.forbes.com/sites/janbruce/2020/01/07/the-future-of-zwork-is-now-embrace-the-uncertainty/?sh=22880ca66f82

Bryan. W.J. n.d. "Quotes." www.goodreads.com/author/quotes/310550. William_Jennings_Bryan

Bryant, A. August 05, 2020. "Ambiguous Times are no Time for Ambiguous Leadership." *Strategy + Business,* www.strategy-business.com/blog/Ambiguous-times-are-no-time-for-ambiguous-leadership?gko=e025c

Bunch, E. March 15, 2021. "How to Deal With Unexpected Anxiety About Life Post-Pandemic." *Well and Good,* www.wellandgood.com/post-pandemic-anxeity/

Burning Glass Technologies. February 2021. "After the Storm: The Jobs and Skills that will Drive the Post-Pandemic Recovery." www.burning-glass.com/wp-content/uploads/2021/02/after_the_storm_recovery_jobs_executive_summary.pdf

Busteed, B. February 25, 2014. "Higher Education's Work Preparation Paradox." *Gallup,* https://news.gallup.com/opinion/gallup/173249/higher-education-work-preparation-paradox.aspx

Cacciattolo, K. May 2015. "Defining Workplace Learning." *European Scientific Journal,* www.researchgate.net/publication/277206749_Defining_Workplace_Learning

Cadsby, T. July 25, 2011. "Why Being Certain Means Being Wrong." *Harvard Business Review,* https://hbr.org/2011/07/why-being-certain-means-being

Carmen, A. May 15, 2020. "Uncertainty Can Be Our Best Friend." *Psychology Today,* www.psychologytoday.com/intl/blog/the-gift-maybe/202005/uncertainty-can-be-our-best-friend?amp

Carr, N. July/August 2008. "Is Google Making Us Stupid?" *The Atlantic,* www.theatlantic.com/magazine/archive/2008/07/is-google-making-us-stupid/306868/

Carroll, L. 1865. "Alice's Adventures in Wonderland." www.open-bks.com/alice-cover.html

Carucci, R. March 30, 2020. "Finding Hope in the Face of a Pandemic." *Forbes,* www.forbes.com/sites/roncarucci/2020/03/30/how-to-help-people-find-real-hope-in-the-face-of-the-pandemic/?sh=19f570b85a1a

Cave, D., E. Bubola, and C. Sang-Hun. May 22, 2012. "Long Slide Looms for World Population, With Sweeping Ramifications." *The New York Times,* www.nytimes.com/2021/05/22/world/global-population-shrinking.html

"Citizenship in a Republic." *Wikipedia,* https://en.wikipedia.org/wiki/Citizenship_in_a_Republic (accessed May 02, 2021).

Chan, K. April 21, 2021. "EU Outlines Ambitious AI Regulations Focused on Risky Uses." *AP,* https://apnews.com/article/technology-business-government-and-politics-artificial-intelligence-data-privacy-5226382bb316f8aad4cbc5637f03a44c

"Chief of Chobani." 60 Minutes, April 09, 2017. www.cbsnews.com/video/chief-of-chobani/

Chihuly, D. n.d. "Biography." https://robinrile.com/contemporary-sculptures/dale-chihuly-biography/

Christensen, C.M., J. Allworth, and K. Dillon. May 15, 2012. "How Will You Measure Your Life?" Hardcover, www.amazon.com/How-Will-Measure-Your-Life/dp/0062102419

Christensen, U.J. December 29, 2020. "How Companies Will Stand Out Post-Pandemic." *Forbes,* www.forbes.com/sites/ulrikjuulchristensen/2021/12/29/how-companies-will-stand-out-post-pandemic/?sh=acf8d412c07e

Church, B. December 18, 2020. "We Should be Less Afraid to be Afraid,' Says Emily Harrington after historic El Capitan climb." *CNN,* www.cnn.com/2020/12/18/sport/emily-harrington-el-capitan-climb-record-cmd-spt-intl/index.html

Church, B. December 18, 2020. "We Should Be Less Afraid to be Afraid,' Says Emily Harrington After Historic El Capitan Climb." *CNN,* www.cnn.com/2020/12/18/sport/emily-harrington-el-capitan-climb-record-cmd-spt-intl/index.html

Clay, R.A. July 01, 2020. "Self-Care has Never Been More Important." *American Psychological Association,* www.apa.org/monitor/2020/07/self-care

Coelho, P. May 10, 2017. "Tweet." https://twitter.com/paulocoelho/status/862336571927908352?lang=en

Cohan, P. January 29, 2021. "4 Ways to Embrace Uncertainty and Ambiguity." *Inc.,* www.inc.com/peter-cohan/4-ways-to-embrace-uncertainty-ambiguity.html

Cohen, R. October 2014. "The Ride of His Life." *Vanity Fair,* www.vanityfair.com/hollywood/2014/09/robert-downey-jr-addiction-children

Colagrossi, M. June 03, 2019. "In the Future, Will We Acquire Skills, Not Degrees?" *Big Think,* https://bigthink.com/personal-growth/skills-degrees?rebelltitem=1#rebelltitem1

Collins, B. June 18, 2018. "Here's What Scott Adams Says About Goals." *Forbes,* www.forbes.com/sites/bryancollinseurope/2018/06/28/scott-adams-goals/?sh=2e77f4e34a2f

Colonel Kail, E.G. August 19, 2013. "Leading Effective in a VUCA Environment: A is for Ambiguity." *The Conference Board,* www.conference-board.org/blog/postdetail.cfm?post=2090

"Coronavirus: How can Society Thrive Post-Pandemic?" *BBC*, November 18, 2020. www.bbc.com/worklife/article/20201118-coronavirus-how-will-it-affect-inequalities-mental-health

Congressional Research Service. 2021. "The U.S. Income Distribution: Trends and Issues." https://fas.org/sgp/crs/misc/R44705.pdf (accessed January 13, 2021).

Covey, S.R. 1989. "The 7 Habits of Highly Effective People: Powerful Lessons in Personal Change." www.amazon.com/Stephen-R-Covey-Effective-Powerful/dp/B00824Z9RU

COVID-19 Dashboard by the Center for Systems Science and Engineering (CSSE) at Johns Hopkins University (JHU) website, https://coronavirus.jhu.edu/map.html (accessed February 28, 2021).

Cowen, T. January 13, 2021. "Brace Yourself for the Next 11 1/2 Months." *Bloomberg*, www.bloomberg.com/opinion/articles/2021-01-13/2021-will-be-better-than-2020-but-far-more-volatile

Cranston, S. November 15, 2020. "Leading in a VUCA World." https://obj.ca/article/authentika-consulting-leading-vuca-world

Crutsinger, M. October 13, 2020. "IMF Envisions a Sharp 4.4 Percent Drop In Global Growth for 2020." *AP*, www.pbs.org/newshour/economy/imf-envisions-a-sharp-4-4-percent-drop-in-global-growth-for-2020.

Daily Plain Dealer, Mrs. Cora L.V. January 15, 1859. "Hatch on Spiritualism: The Law of God a Unit, Quote Page 2, Column 3, Cleveland, Ohio." https://quoteinvestigator.com/tag/dolly-parton/

"Dame Helen Mirren Shares Her '5 Top Rules for a Happy Life' with Grads." www.bbcamerica.com/anglophenia/2017/05/watch-dame-helen-mirren-shares-her-5-top-rules-for-a-happy-life-with-grads

Damme, D.V. n.d. "How Closely is the Distribution of Skills Related to Countries' Overall Level of Social Inequality and Economic Prosperity." *Organization for Economic and Community Development*, www.oecd.org/education/skills-beyond-school/EDUNAEC1.pdf

Dargis, D. May 15, 2016. "A Word With: Steven Spielberg." *The New York Times*, www.nytimes.com/2016/05/17/movies/a-word-with-steven-spielberg.html

"Data Driven: What Students Need to Succeed in a Rapidly Changing Business World." PwC white paper dated February 2015.

Davis, D.M., and J.A. Hayes. July/August 2012. "What are the Benefits Of Mindfulness." American Psychological Association, www.apa.org/monitor/2012/07-08/ce-corner

Deaton, A.V. 2018. "VUCA Tools for a VUCA World: Developing Leaders and Teams for Sustainable Results." www.amazon.com/VUCA-Tools-World-Developing-

Deloitte Global Human Capital Trends. 2019. "Leading the Social Enterprise: Reinvent with a Human Focus." www2.deloitte.com/content/dam/Deloitte/cz/Documents/human-capital/cz-hc-trends-reinvent-with-human-focus.pdf

Deloitte. 2021. "Agility: The Antidote to Complexity." Global Chief Procurement Officer Survey, www2.deloitte.com/content/dam/insights/articles/6838_Agility-the-antidote-to-complexity/DI_Agility-the-antidote-to-complexity.pdf (accessed April 2021).

DeSimone, R., and J. Robison. January 23, 2021. "3 Employee Development Interventions for 2021." *Gallup*, www.gallup.com/workplace/328715/employee-development-interventions-2021.aspx

Diamond, A. November 28, 2017. "It's Never Too Late: 3 Women on Second Chances and Changing Careers." *Repeller*, https://repeller.com/how-to-make-a-career-change/

Díaz, S., and M. Turits. n.d. "How the World has an Unexpected 'Chance to Reset'." *BBC*, www.bbc.com/worklife/bespoke/the-life-project/how-the-world-has-had-an-unexpected-chance-to-reset/

Dienstbier, R.A. 1989. "Arousal and Physiological Toughness: Implications for Mental and Physical Health." *Psychological Review* 96, no. 1, pp. 84–1000. https://philpapers.org/rec/DIEAAP-2

Dillon, J.D. August 15, 2017. "In Real Life: Self-Directed Learning Can Only Work If." *Learning Solutions*, https://tinyurl.com/yupf6ej5

Doyle, B. 2019. "The Call: The Desire to Finish Strong." www.amazon.com/Call-Desire-Finish-Strong/dp/1545657378/ref=tmm_pap_swatch_0?_encoding=UTF8&qid=&sr=

Duckworth, A., et al. 2007. "Grit: Perseverance and Passion for Long-Term Goals." *Journal of Personality and Social Psychology*, https://psycnet.apa.org/record/2007-07951-009

Edelman, M.W. 1993. "The Measure of Our Success: A Letter to My Children and Yours." www.amazon.com/Measure-Our-Success-Letter-Children/dp/0060975466/ref=tmm_pap_swatch_0?_encoding=UTF8&qid=&sr=

"Eisenhower's Urgent/Important Principle." n.d. www.mindtools.com/pages/article/newHTE_91.htm

Eggersten, C. June 19, 2015. "The Nightmare of 'Jaws': 10 On-Set Disasters that Plagued Spielberg's 1975 Classic." *Uproxx*, https://uproxx.com/hitfix/jaws-turns-40-10-times-the-production-was-scarier-than-the-movie/

"Emerging From a "VUCA" World—How Sales Leaders Can Set a Course for Less Stress in 2021." January 25, 2021. Press Release, https://tinyurl.com/2bh7byaa

Emrich, M. December 17, 2020. "Being a Successful Leader in Today's VUCA World." *American Management Association*, www.amanet.org/articles/being-a-successful-leader-in-todays-vuca-world/

Estes, J. March 29, 2021. "Tackling Post-Pandemic CX Challenges With a Focus on Empathy." *CMS Wire*, www.cmswire.com/customer-experience/tackling-post-pandemic-cx-challenges-with-a-focus-on-empathy/

Fagerholm, M. July 29, 2016. "Miss Sharon Jones!." *Roger Ebert*, www.rogerebert.com/reviews/miss-sharon-jones-2016

Farina, D. n.d. Quotes located at www.azquotes.com/author/4663-Dennis_Farina

Federer, R. April 03, 2017. "Never Stop Improving." *Goalcoast*, https://goalcast.com/2017/04/03/roger-federer-never-stop-improving/

Fitzsimmons, E.G. December 02, 2018. "Why Are Taxi Drivers in New York Killing Themselves?" *The New York Times*, www.nytimes.com/2018/12/02/nyregion/taxi-drivers-suicide-nyc.html

Flanagan, K., and D. Gregory. 2019. "The 12 Skills to Future Proof Yourself, Your Team and Your Kids." *Wiley*, www.amazon.com/Forever-Skills-Futureproof-Yourself-Your/dp/0730359174#reader_0730359174

Flood, A. January 04, 2015. "Watership Down author Richard Adams: I Just Can't Do Humans." *The Guardian*, www.theguardian.com/books/2015/jan/04/richard-adams-watership-down-interview?elq=a5d0b06514524b5eb363e56655e022d1&elqCampaignId=12850&elqaid=15185&elqat=1&elqTrackId=e568573133814ad0be32be790d2a2c79

Flood, A. July 22, 2014. "Judy Blume Interview." *The Guardian*, www.theguardian.com/books/2014/jul/11/judy-blume-interview-forever-writer-children-young-adults

For information about the Alliance visit www.markle.org/alliance

For more information on these three trends and the top 15 technologies of the near future, read "Latest Technology Trends That Will Impact Businesses in 2021." www.mobileappdaily.com/future-technology-trends (accessed May 20, 2021).

For the Latest Data on Global Internet Penetration visit www.internetworldstats.com/stats14.htm (accessed March 01, 2021).

Fox, M. December 19, 2015. "Kurt Masur, Conductor Who Transformed New York Philharmonic, Dies at 88." *The New York Times*, www.nytimes.com/2015/12/20/arts/music/kurt-masur-new-york-philharmonic-conductor-dies.html

Friedman, T.L. October 20, 2020. "After the Pandemic, A Revolution in Education and Work Awaits." *The New York Times*, www.nytimes.com/2020/10/20/opinion/covid-education-work.html

"From Bank Robber to Law Professor." *60 Minutes*, October 12, 2017. www.cbsnews.com/video/from-bank-robber-to-law-professor/

Fuchs, M., J. Messner, and R. Sok. 2020. Leadership in a VUCA World, www.amazon.com/Leadership-Vuca-World-Michael-Fuchs/dp/1950576116/ref=sr_1_3?dchild=1&keywords=VUCA&qid=1616423806&sr=8-3 Sustainable/dp/0692074945/ref=sr_1_2?dchild=1&keywords=VUCA&qid=1616423602&sr=8-2

"Full Metal Jacket Interview." *YouTube*, June 21, 2017. www.youtube.com/watch?v=ZjVLAdNlrNs

Gaiman, N. 2008. "The Graveyard Book." www.amazon.com/Graveyard-Book-Neil-Gaiman/dp/0060530928/ref=tmm_hrd_swatch_0?_encoding=UTF8&qid=1621781492&sr=8-1

Gardner, D. 2009. "The Science of Fear: How the Culture of Fear Manipulates Your Brain." www.amazon.com/Science-Fear-Culture-Manipulates-Brain/dp/B0030EG0OS/ref=pd_lpo_14_t_1/144-4533982-5966950?_encoding=UTF8&pd_rd_i=B0030EG0OS&pd_rd_r=32c7f17a-b0a2-4fb0-8128-0539291de364&pd_rd_w=6dWov&pd_rd_wg=FzIi4&pf_rd_p=a0d6e967-6561-454c-84f8-2ce2c92b79a6&pf_rd_r=NYGJCFXYW356F989255X&psc=1&refRID=NYGJCFXYW356F989255X

Garton, E., and M. Mankins. December 01, 2020. "The Pandemic Is Widening a Corporate Productivity Gap." *Harvard Business Review*, https://hbr.org/2020/12/the-pandemic-is-widening-a-corporate-productivity-gap

Gaskell, A. May 11, 2020. "Is A Blurred Work-Life Balance The New Normal?" *Forbes*, www.forbes.com/sites/adigaskell/2020/05/11/is-a-blurred-work-life-balance-the-new-normal/?sh=7a66a7ca1813

General Casey, G.W., Jr. U.S. Army (Retired). n.d. "Leading in a VUCA World." *Cornell College of Business white paper*, https://tinyurl.com/3v9jtuzy

Gigerenzer, G. 2004. "Dread Risk, September 11, and Fatal Traffic Accidents." *Psychological Science*, https://citeseerx.ist.psu.edu/viewdoc/download?doi=10.1.1.398.4395&rep=rep1&type=pdf

Gilman, D. 2017. "Outsmarting VUCA: Achieving Success in a Volatile, Uncertain, Complex, & Ambiguous World." www.amazon.com/Outsmarting-VUCA-Achieving-Uncertain-Ambiguous/dp/1599326205/ref=sr_1_5?dchild=1&keywords=VUCA&qid=1616423731&sr=8-5

Global Risks Report. 2021. "World Economic Forum and Marsh McLennan." www.mmc.com/insights/publications/2021/january/global-risks-report.html

Global Sports Website. www.goglobalsports.org/brian-and-connie-doyle/

Gobrin, A. February 23, 2021. "The Future of Work: How to Prepare for the Post-Pandemic Workplace." *Forbes*. https://tinyurl.com/2x4dwmms

Gobrin, A. May 06, 2020. "How A Global Crisis Stands to Strengthen Our Workforce." *Forbes*, https://tinyurl.com/2x4dwmms

Goggins, D. March 19, 2018. "Facebook Post." www.facebook.com/514917602052937/photos/a.653481068196589/768834569994571/

Goggins, D. November 11, 2017. "How to Conquer Your Mind and Embrace the Suck." *Youtube*, www.youtube.com/watch?v=_J_bOqPhuZA

Goldberg, A. January 28, 2021. "Workforce Mobility 2021." *Weichert*, www.weichertworkforcemobility.com/blog-post/workforce-mobility-2021-moving-talent-in-a-vuca-world-part-one/

Goldberg, A. January 28, 2021. "Workforce Mobility 2021: Moving Talent in a VUCA World (Part One)." *Weichert*, www.weichertworkforcemobility.com/blog-post/workforce-mobility-2021-moving-talent-in-a-vuca-world-part-one/

Gould, E. March 05, 2021. "Jobs Report Shows More Than 25 Million Workers are Directly Harmed by the COVID Labor Market." *Economic Policy Institute*, www.epi.org/press/jobs-report-shows-more-than-25-million-workers-are-directly-harmed-by-the-covid-labor-market-congress-must-pass-the-full-1-9-trillion-relief-package-immediately/

Gould, E. March 05, 2021. "Jobs Report Shows More Than 25 Million Workers are Directly Harmed by the COVID Labor Market." *Economic Policy Institute*, www.epi.org/press/jobs-report-shows-more-than-25-million-workers-are-directly-harmed-by-the-covid-labor-market-congress-must-pass-the-full-1-9-trillion-relief-package-immediately/

Govaert, A., and M. Cao. July 22, 2020. "Strategically Influencing an Uncertain Future." *Nature*, www.nature.com/articles/s41598-020-69006-x

Graham, K. https://en.wikipedia.org/wiki/Katharine_Graham#cite_note-33 (accessed May 21, 2021).

Greenway, T. April 26, 2018. "Women Who Inspire Us: Meet Ashley Lamothe." *Chicken Wire*, https://thechickenwire.chick-fil-a.com/inside-chick-fil-a/women-who-inspire-us-meet-ashley-derby

Gross, T. May 12, 2021. "From 'Designing Women' to 'Hacks', Jean Smart's Career Is Still Going Strong." *NPR*, www.npr.org/2021/05/12/996175170/from-designing-women-to-hacks-jean-smarts-career-is-still-going-strong

Guengerich, G. October 16, 2015. "The Four Stages of Desire: From Everything to One Thing." *Psychology Today*, www.psychologytoday.com/us/blog/the-search-meaning/201510/the-four-stages-desire-everything-one-thing

Guse, C. January 30, 2020. "Driving NYC Taxis Out of Business: How Uber and Lyft Doomed the Once-Solid Yellow Cab Industry." *New York Daily News*, www.nydailynews.com/new-york/ny-medallion-foreclosures-taxi-bailout-plan-uber-lyft-20200130-s2mjkhjubzgptdxasoxddwdote-story.html

Guse, C. January 30, 2020. "Driving NYC Taxis Out of Business: How Uber and Lyft Doomed the Once-Solid Yellow Cab Industry." *New York Daily News*, www.nydailynews.com/new-york/ny-medallion-foreclosures-taxi-bailout-plan-uber-lyft-20200130-s2mjkhjubzgptdxasoxddwdote-story.html

Gutierrez, K. May 24, 2017. "The Advantages of Self-Directed Learning in the Workplace." *LinkedIn*, www.linkedin.com/pulse/advantages-self-directed-learning-workplace-karla-gutierrez/

Haden, J. January 02, 2018. "An Almost Guaranteed Way to Achieve Every Goal You Set This Year." *Inc.*, www.inc.com/jeff-haden/an-almost-guaranteed-way-to-achieve-every-goal-you-set-this-year.html

Hammond, C. March 18, 2014. "Why we choke under pressure." *BBC*, www.bbc.com/future/article/20140319-why-we-choke-under-pressure

Harrington, S.J., and C.P. Ruppel. December, 1999. "Telecommuting: A Test of Trust, Competing Values, and Relative Advantage." In *IEEE Transactions on Professional Communication* 42, no. 4, pp. 223–239.

Hartley, D. October 21, 2020. "The Porcupine Dilemma: What Sigmund Freud Knew." *Psychology Today,* www.psychologytoday.com/us/blog/machiavellians-gulling-the-rubes/202010/the-porcupine-dilemma-what-sigmund-freud-knew

Haynie, S. April 27, 2021. "How Self-Awareness Takes Team Performance to New Heights in 2021." *ADT,* www.td.org/atd-blog/how-self-awareness-takes-team-performance-to-new-heights-in-2021

Hazel, M., and N. Paula. 1986. "Possible Selves." *American Psychologist* 41, pp. 954–969. www.researchgate.net/publication/232565363_Possible_Selves/citation/download

He, E. September 22, 2020. "Why Learning Is the Future of Work." *Forbes,* www.forbes.com/sites/emilyhe/2020/09/22/why-learning-is-the-future-of-work/?sh=37d3843155ac

Hennessy, J. January/February 2002. "Embracing the Need to Learn and Relearn." *Stanford Magazine,* https://stanfordmag.org/contents/embracing-the-need-to-learn-and-relearn

Hepps, T. July 24, 2014. "What We Can Learn from Socrates about Oral History." http://b.treelines.com/who-replaced-my-memory/

Herrera, C., and J. Carlson. n.d. "Change Management: The Impact of Now." *Work Design,* www.workdesign.com/2019/10/change-management-the-impact-of-now/

Herrera, T. December 01, 2019. "Thinking About a Job or Career Change? Read This." *The New York Times,* www.nytimes.com/2019/12/01/smarter-living/thinking-about-a-job-or-career-change-read-this.html

Herrera, T. February 06, 2021. "Remember: What You Do is Not Who You Are." *The New York Times,* www.nytimes.com/2021/02/06/style/work-life-balance-tips-pandemic.html

Hirsch, A.S. July 10, 2020. "Empowering Employees Before, During and After the Pandemic." *SHRM,* www.shrm.org/resourcesandtools/hr-topics/employee-relations/pages/empowering-employees-before-during-and-after-the-pandemic.aspx

History of the Peloponnesian War, translated from the Greek of Thucydides. by William Smith, 1836. https://books.google.com/books?id=1e4LAAAA YAAJ&printsec=frontcover&source=gbs_ge_summary_r&cad=0#v=one page&q&f=false

"History Quotes." n.d. www.keepinspiring.me/history-quotes/

Honnold, A., and D. Roberts. 2015. Alone on the Wall, www.amazon.com/dp/0393247627/ref=blogs_omni_link_20151125noWALLal

Horn, M.B., and B. Moesta. 2020. "A Not So Tidy Narrative." *Inside Higher Ed,* January 06, 2020. www.insidehighered.com/views/2020/01/06/pervasive-narrative-students-are-going-college-just-get-job-isnt-always-so-true

Hougaard, R., J. Carter, and N. Hobson. December 04, 2020. "Self-Compassion is Necessary-But Not Sufficient." *Harvard Business Review,* https://hbr.org/2020/12/compassionate-leadership-is-necessary-but-not-sufficient

Houle, D. October 11, 2020. "Introduction to VUCA: the Best Leadership for this Decade." *Medium,* https://medium.com/the-2020s-decade/introduction-to-vuca-the-best-leadership-for-this-decade-b68945960cfc

How I Climbed a 3,000-Foot Vertical Cliff—Without Ropes: Alex Honnold (Transcript), March 16, 2019. https://singjupost.com/how-i-climbed-a-3000-foot-vertical-cliff-without-ropes-alex-honnold-transcript/

Howkins, J. 2013. "The Creative Economy: How People Make Money from Ideas." www.amazon.com/Creative-Economy-People-Money-Ideas/dp/0141977035

https://goodreads.com/quotes/61242-i-pay-no-attention-whatever-to-anybody-s-praise-or-blame

https://sbctc.instructure.com/courses/1934284/pages/3-dot-4-a-receptive-mindset?module_item_id=41213570

https://sbctc.instructure.com/courses/1934284/pages/3-dot-4-a-receptive-mindset

Huber, M.F. June 09, 2017. "A Brief History of the Sub-4-Minute Mile." *Outside,* www.outsideonline.com/2191776/brief-history-sub-4-minute-mile

Hughes, H. October 16, 2018. "Sharon Jones Is the 21st Century's Godmother of Soul." *NPR,* https://www.npr.org/2018/10/16/655847988/sharon-jones-is-the-21st-centurys-godmother-of-soul

Huston, M. January 02, 2021. "Going the Distance (and Then Some)." *Psychology Today,* www.psychologytoday.com/us/articles/202101/going-the-distance-and-then-some

Huxley, A. 1958. "Collected Essays." www.amazon.com/Collected-Essays-Aldous-Huxley/dp/B001MAMC1W

Hyder, S. May 04, 2021. "The Future of Work in Post-Pandemic America." *Forbes,* www.forbes.com/sites/shamahyder/2021/05/04/the-future-of-work-in-post-pandemic-america/?sh=7a44793621e2

IBM. 2021. "CEO Study: Find Your Essential: How to Thrive in a Post-Pandemic Reality." www.ibm.com/thought-leadership/institute-business-value/report/ceo

Impact of the Coronavirus Pandemic on the Global Economy—Statistics & Facts, published by Statista Research Department, www.statista.com/topics/6139/covid-19-impact-on-the-global-economy/ (accessed February 23, 2021).

"In Pandemic Era's Isolation, Meaning of 'Self-Care' Evolves." November 24, 2020. www.voanews.com/covid-19-pandemic/pandemic-eras-isolation-meaning-self-care-evolves

International Monetary Fund (IMF), World Economic Outlook. October 2020. "A Long and Difficult Ascent." www.imf.org/en/Publications/WEO/Issues/2020/09/30/world-economic-outlook-october-2020

"Is Microsoft Office Proficiency Still Needed Nowadays?" January 12, 2021. www.globaltrademag.com/is-microsoft-office-proficiency-still-needed-nowadays/

"Is This Working?: Pulse of the American Worker Survey: Special Report." *Prudential,* March 2021. file:///C:/Users/micha/AppData/Local/Temp/AWS_Is-This-Working_Fact Sheet_FINAL.pdf

Isay, D. May 13, 2020. "Now Is the Time to Ask Your Loved Ones About their Lives." *New York Times,* www.nytimes.com/2020/05/13/opinion/quarantine-storycorps-interview.html

Jain, N. April 28, 2021. "Prepare for Uncertainities." *The Hindu,* www.thehindu.com/education/how-budding-leaders-or-manager-can-prepare-for-an-uncertain-future/article34431033.ece

James, M. September 01, 2006. "React vs Respond." *Psychology Today,* www.psychologytoday.com/intl/blog/focus-forgiveness/201609/react-vs-respond?amp

Jantz, G.L. January 03, 2017. "Patience: A Wise Response to Life." *Psychology Today,* www.psychologytoday.com/us/blog/hope-relationships/201701/patience-wise-response-life

Jezard, A. June 01, 2018. "The 3 Key Skill Sets for the Workers of 2030." www.weforum.org/agenda/2018/06/the-3-skill-sets-workers-need-to-develop-between-now-and-2030/

Jones, B.T. February 22, 2021. "The Future of Work: Workplace Trends for 2021 and Beyond." *National Law Review,* www.natlawreview.com/article/future-work-workplace-trends-2021-and-beyond

Jones, L., D. Palumbo, and D. Brown. January 24, 2021. "Coronavirus: How the pandemic has Changed the World Economy." *BBC,* www.bbc.com/news/business-51706225.

Kahneman, D. 2011. "Thinking, Fast and Slow." www.amazon.com/Thinking-Fast-Slow-Daniel-Kahneman/dp/0374533555

Kane, G.C., R. Nanda, A. Phillips, and J. Copulsky. February 10, 2021. "Redesigning the Post-Pandemic Workplace." *MIT Sloan,* https://sloanreview.mit.edu/article/redesigning-the-post-pandemic-workplace/

Kaufman, A. September 29, 2010. "Top Science Fiction Novels of All Time." http://top-science-fiction-novels.com/dune-frank-herbert/

Kenny, G. July 08, 2020. "'Inmate #1: The Rise of Danny Trejo' Review: Prison, Recovery, Stardom." *The New York Times,* www.nytimes.com/2020/07/08/movies/inmate-1-the-rise-of-danny-trejo-review.html

Keynes, J.M. 1936. "The General Theory of Employment, Interest and Money." www.marxists.org/reference/subject/economics/keynes/general-theory/preface.htm

Khan, P. July 06, 2020. "Lifelong Learning Post-Covid—Creating Pathways to Success." *LinkedIn,* https://tinyurl.com/5ye484zw

King, B.J. September 13, 2012. "For How Long Have we Been Human?" *NPR*, www.npr.org/sections/13.7/2012/09/11/160934187/for-how-long-have-we-been-human

Kinney, D. January 18, 2021. "The Mathematical Case Against Blaming People for their Misfortune." *Psyche*, https://psyche.co/ideas/the-mathematical-case-against-blaming-people-for-their-misfortune

Knowles, M. 1975. "Self-Directed Learning a Guide for Learners and Teachers." https://journals.sagepub.com/doi/10.1177/105960117700200220

Kochhar, R. March 18, 2021. "The Pandemic Stalls Growth in the Global Middle Class, Pushes Poverty Up Sharply." *Pew Research Center*, www.pewresearch.org/global/2021/03/18/the-pandemic-stalls-growth-in-the-global-middle-class-pushes-poverty-up-sharply/

Koehn, N. April 03, 2020. "Real Leaders Are Forged in Crisis." *Harvard Business Review*, https://hbr.org/2020/04/real-leaders-are-forged-in-crisis

Kolakowski, N. September 10, 2019. "Elon Musk Wants You to Learn Soft Skills to Keep Your Job." *Dice*, https://insights.dice.com/2019/09/10/elon-musk-learn-soft-skills-keep-job/

Kropp, B. January 14, 2021. "9 Trends That Will Shape Work in 2021 and Beyond." *Harvard Business Review*. https://hbr.org/2021/01/9-trends-that-will-shape-work-in-2021-and-beyond

Kurtz, A. January 08, 2021. "The US Economy Lost 140,000 Jobs in December. All of Them Were Held By Women." *CNN*, www.cnn.com/2021/01/08/economy/women-job-losses-pandemic/index.html

Lau, Y. January 20, 2021. "Soft Skills are Essential to the Future of Work." *Forbes*, www.forbes.com/sites/forbeshumanresourcescouncil/2021/01/20/soft-skills-are-essential-to-the-future-of-work/?sh=4e3fb4ef1341

Lazear, E.P. August 04, 2020. "Growing Wage Inequality Is Caused by Growing Skill Inequality." *National Review*, www.nationalreview.com/2020/08/growing-wage-inequality-is-caused-by-growing-skill-inequality/

Leigh, D. November 24, 2016. "Aaron Eckhart: 'I'm 48. For 20 years I've Made Mistakes'." *Guardian*, www.theguardian.com/culture/2016/nov/24/aaron-eckhart-sully-bleed-for-this-20-years-made-mistakes

Levitz, J. April 11, 2021. "Covid-19 Was a Wake-Up Call, Leading Many to Make Lifestyle and Career Changes." *The Wall Street Journal*, www.wsj.com/articles/covid-19-was-a-wake-up-call-leading-many-to-make-lifestyle-and-career-changes-11618133400

Lieberman, M. March 02, 2021. "Top U.S. Companies: These Are the Skills Students Need in a Post-Pandemic World." *Ed Week*, www.edweek.org/technology/top-u-s-companies-these-are-the-skills-students-need-in-a-post-pandemic-world/2021/03

Lillard, D. December 12, 2020. *Instagram post*, www.instagram.com/p/CIuPO9hg9pi/?hl=en

"Living in a VUCA World: How Modern Leaders are Evolving to Navigate Disruption." February 24, 2020. www.ie.edu/exponential-learning/blog/leadership-strategy/living-vuca-world-modern-leaders/

Liu, J. April 19, 2021. "1 in 4 Workers is Considering Quitting Their Job After the Pandemic—Here's Why." *CNBC*, www.cnbc.com/2021/04/19/1-in-4-workers-is-considering-quitting-their-job-after-the-pandemic.html

Lombardozzi, C. 2020. "Self-Directed Learning: Essential Strategy for a Rapidly Changing World." *The Learning Guild*, https://learningsolutionsmag.com/articles/why-self-directed-learning-is-crucial-today

Long, H. May 07, 2021. "It's Not a Labor Shortage." *The Washington Post*, www.washingtonpost.com/business/2021/05/07/jobs-report-labor-shortage-analysis/

"'Look for Skills, Not Credentials': Beth Cobert on Tapping into US Talent." February 26, 2021 https://tinyurl.com/y4u9h84b

Ludden, D. November 16, 2016. "Deciding, Fast and Slow." *Psychology Today*, www.psychologytoday.com/us/blog/talking-apes/201611/deciding-fast-and-slow

Luhby, T., and A. Tappe. February 02, 2021. "American Jobs won't Return to Pre-Pandemic Levels Until 2024, CBO Says." *CNN*, www.cnn.com/2021/02/01/economy/cbo-economy-projections-jobs-gdp/index.html

MacCarthy, M., and K. Propp. May 04, 2021. "Machines Learn that Brussels Writes the Rules: The EU's New AI Regulation." *Brookings*, www.brookings.edu/blog/techtank/2021/05/04/machines-learn-that-brussels-writes-the-rules-the-eus-new-ai-regulation/

Madison, K. Summer 2015. "Intentional Walk: Brian Doyle—An Extended Baseball Family." *Inside Pitch*, https://abca.org/magazine/2015-3-Summer/Intentional_Walk_Brian_Doyle_An_Extended_Baseball_Family.aspx

Malcolm Gladwell, Blink: The Power of Thinking Without Thinking, 2005. www.amazon.com/Blink-Power-Thinking-Without/dp/0316172324/ref=tmm_hrd_swatch_0?_encoding=UTF8&qid=1618866138&sr=8-1

Mandino, O. 1975. "The Greatest Miracle in World." www.amazon.com/Greatest-Miracle-World-Og-Mandino/dp/0553122185/ref=tmm_pap_swatch_0?_encoding=UTF8&qid=&sr=

Marczi, M. May, 27, 2020. "Mel Blount: 'You Cannot Write the History of the Pittsburgh Steelers Without Bill Nunn.'" *Steelers Depot*, https://steelersdepot.com/2020/05/mel-blount-you-cannot-write-the-history-of-the-pittsburgh-steelers-without-bill-nunn/

Martel, Y. 2002. "Life of Pi." www.amazon.com/Life-Pi-Yann-Martel/dp/0151008116/ref=tmm_hrd_swatch_0?_encoding=UTF8&qid=&sr=

Martin, K. 2012. "The Outstanding Organization: Generate Business Results by Eliminating Chaos and Building the Foundation for Everyday Excellence." www.amazon.com/Outstanding-Organization-Eliminating-Foundation-Excellence/dp/0071782370

Martin, L. May 24, 2019. "Alex Honnold: Who is the Climber Who Scaled Yosemite's El Capitan in Free Solo?" *iNews*, https://inews.co.uk/culture/film/alex-honnold-free-solo-el-capitan-yosemite-climber-documentary-film-channel-4-235423

"Matt Murray made a Heartwarming Gesture to Jacob Markstrom after his Father Passed Away." n.d. www.bardown.com/matt-murray-made-a-heartwarming-gesture-to-jacob-markstrom-after-his-father-passed-away-1.1405080

Maxwell, J. January 14, 2015. "It All Comes Down to What You Do Daily." *Blog post*, www.johnmaxwell.com/blog/it-all-comes-down-to-what-you-do-daily/

McChrystal, S., and C. Fussell. March 23, 2020. "What 9/11 Taught us About Leadership in a Crisis." *The New York Times*, www.nytimes.com/2020/03/23/opinion/coronavirus-mcchrystal-leadership.html

McEvers, K. May 10, 2017. "Don't Be Fooled: 'Generation Wealth' Is More About Wanting Than Having." *NPR*, www.npr.org/2017/05/10/527429299/dont-be-fooled-generation-wealth-is-more-about-wanting-than-having

McKinsey Global Institute. 2021. "The Future of Work After COVID-19." www.mckinsey.com/featured-insights/future-of-work/the-future-of-work-after-covid-19 (accessed February 18, 2021).

McKinsey. May 01, 2020. "Tuning in, Turning Outward: Cultivating Compassionate Leadership in a Crisis." www.mckinsey.com/business-functions/organization/our-insights/tuning-in-turning-outward-cultivating-compassionate-leadership-in-a-crisis

Melnyk, J. May 05, 2021. "Opinion: Employers need to get with the Post-Pandemic Work Program or Lose Star Employees." *Market Watch*, www.marketwatch.com/story/employers-need-to-get-with-the-post-pandemic-work-program-or-lose-star-employees-11620182891

Menand, L. November 27, 2005. "Everybody Is an Expert." *New Yorker*.

"Mental Health, Substance Use, and Suicidal Ideation During the COVID-19 Pandemic—United States, June 24–30, 2020." August 14, 2020. Centers for Disease Control. www.cdc.gov/mmwr/volumes/69/wr/mm6932a1.htm

Michel de Montaigne. n.d. "The Complete Essays." www.goodreads.com/quotes/29637-there-is-nothing-more-notable-in-author-socrates-275648-than-that-he

Miglani, B. 2013. "Embrace the Chaos: How India Taught Me to Stop Overthinking and Start Living." www.amazon.com/Embrace-Chaos-Taught-Overthinking-Living/dp/1609948254/ref=sr_1_1?dchild=1&keywords=embrace+the+chaos&qid=1618431171&s=books&sr=1-1

"Mile Run World Record Progression." *Wikipedia*. https://en.wikipedia.org/wiki/Mile_run_world_record_progression

Miller, J. December 27, 2016. "Inside Carrie Fisher's Difficult Upbringing with Famous Parents." *Vanity Fair*, www.vanityfair.com/style/2016/12/carrie-fisher-parents-debbie-reynolds-eddie-hollywood

Miller, K. December 19, 2019. "Leadership Under Pressure: 3 Strategies for Keeping Calm During a Crisis." *Harvard Business School blog*, https://online. hbs.edu/blog/post/leadership-under-pressure

Moon, R. June 03, 2020. "Why the Best Post-COVID-19 Leaders Will Embrace Ambiguity." *Think Set Magazine*, https://thinksetmag.com/insights/moon-covid-leadership-culture

Moran, G. October 27, 2020. "6 Skills Employees will Need in the Post-Pandemic Marketplace." *Fast Company*, www.fastcompany.com/90568262/6-skills-employees-will-need-in-the-post-pandemic-workplace

"Moving Beyond Remote: Workplace Transformation in the Wake of COVID-19." *Slack*. October 07, 2020. https://slack.com/intl/en-ca/blog/collaboration/workplace-transformation-in-the-wake-of-covid-19

Neff, K. February 17, 2016. "Don't Fall into the Self-Esteem Trap: Try a Little Self-Kindness." *Mindful*, www.mindful.org/dont-fall-into-the-self-esteem-trap-try-a-little-self-kindness/

Newman, J. November 19, 2016. "Sharon Jones, Soul and Funk Singer With Dap-Kings, Dead at 60." *Rolling Stone*, www.rollingstone.com/music/music-news/sharon-jones-soul-and-funk-singer-with-dap-kings-dead-at-60-112212/

Nichols, C., S.C. Hayden, and C. Trendler. April 02, 2020. "4 Behaviors that Help Leaders Manage a Crisis." *Harvard Business Review*, https://hbr.org/2020/04/4-behaviors-that-help-leaders-manage-a-crisis

Nicholson, K. February 18, 2021. "Mental Health Screenings and Studies Show Big Jumps in Anxiety, Depression During the Pandemic." *The Denver Post*, www.denverpost.com/2021/02/18/mental-health-colorado-pandemic-anxiety-depression

"Ninth International Forum on Project Management: In the Pandemic's New Normal, Enterprises Need to Go Beyond Agility." Press Release, April 26, 2021. www.prnewswire.com/news-releases/ninth-international-forum-on-project-management-in-the-pandemics-new-normal-enterprises-need-to-go-beyond-agility-301276847.html

Nussbaum, B. June 01, 2003. "Ubuntu: Reflections of a South African on Our Common Humanity." *Reflections: The Sol Journal*, www.researchgate.net/publication/237672969_Ubuntu_Reflections_of_a_South_African_on_Our_Common_Humanity/citation/download

Pace, E. February 11, 1992. "Alex Haley, 70, Author of 'Roots' Dies." *The New York Times*, www.nytimes.com/1992/02/11/books/alex-haley-70-author-of-roots-dies.html

Panchal, N., R. Kamal, C. Cox, and R. Garfield. February 10, 2021. "The Implications of COVID-19 for Mental Health and Substance Use." *KFF*, www.kff.org/coronavirus-covid-19/issue-brief/the-implications-of-covid-19-for-mental-health-and-substance-use/

Pappas, P. 2021. "Bravey: Chasing Dreams, Befriending Pain, and Other Big Ideas." www.amazon.com/Bravey-Chasing-Dreams-Befriending-Other/dp/1984801120

Parker, R.B. n.d. "Interview." *The Strand Magazine*, https://strandmag.com/the-magazine/interviews/robert-b-parker/

Parker, S.K., C. Knight, and A. Keller. July 30, 2020. "Remote Managers are Having Trust Issues." *Harvard Business Review*, https://hbr.org/2020/07/remote-managers-are-having-trust-issues

Parker-Pope, P. July 07, 2016. "Runners on Film: Alexi Pappas Makes More Movies." *New York Times*, https://well.blogs.nytimes.com/2016/07/07/runners-on-film-alexi-pappas-makes-more-movies/

Parrott, C. September 10, 2020. "Be Comfortable With Being Uncomfortable: The Lesson of Covid-19." *School Social Work Association of America*, www.sswaa.org/post/be-comfortable-with-being-uncomfortable-the-lesson-of-covid-19

Pauley. J. May 12, 2019. ""Jeopardy!" Host Alex Trebek on his Cancer Diagnosis." *CBS News*, www.cbsnews.com/news/jeopardy-host-alex-trebek-on-his-cancer-diagnosis/

Perry, T. 2007. "Don't Make a Black Woman Take Off Her Earrings: Madea's Uninhibited Commentaries on Love and Life." https://amazon.com/Dont-Make-Black-Woman-Earrings/dp/1594482403

Petrow, S. October 08, 2020. "Uncertainty Is Hope." *The New York Times,* www.nytimes.com/2020/10/08/well/live/uncertainty-is-hope.html

Pichai, S. March 11, 2021. "Career Certificates and More Ways We're Helping Job Seekers." *Google blog*, https://blog.google/outreach-initiatives/grow-with-google/career-certificates/

Pilon, A. December 08, 2020. "SCORE Looks at Impact of COVID-19 on Small Business in the U.S." *Small Business Trends*, https://smallbiztrends.com/2020/12/score-survey-covid-impact-small-business.html

Pir, S. January 20, 2021. "Going Forward With Imagination: Workplace Trends of 2021 and Why HR Is Called to Action." *Forbes*, www.forbes.com/sites/sesilpir/2021/01/20/going-forward-with-imagination-workplace-trends-of-2021-and-why-hr-is-called-to-action/?sh=1337867a4429

Popova, M. n.d. "Theodore Roosevelt on the Cowardice of Cynicism and the Courage to Create Rather Than Tear Down." *Brain Pickings*, www.brainpickings.org/2018/04/30/theodore-roosevelt-arena-cynicism-critic/

Project Implicit web site located at https://implicit.harvard.edu/implicit/education.html

Prophet of Progress: Selections from the Speeches of Charles F. Kettering, Edited by T. A. Boyd, Speech Title: Opportunities Unlimited, E. P. Dutton and Company, New York. https://quoteinvestigator.com/2017/08/21/tomorrow/#note-16727-1

Pryor, R., and J. Bright. 2012. "The Chaos Theory of Careers: A New Perspective on Working in the Twenty-First Century." www.amazon.com/Chaos-Theory-Careers-Perspective-Twenty-First-dp-0415551889/dp/0415551889/ref=mt_other?_encoding=UTF8&me=&qid=

Rainie, L., and J. Anderson. May 03, 2017. "The Future of Jobs and Jobs Training." *Pew Research Center,* www.pewresearch.org/internet/2017/05/03/the-future-of-jobs-and-jobs-training/

Ralston, A. 2005. "Between a Rock and a Hard Place." www.amazon.com/Between-Rock-Hard-Place-Ralston/dp/074349282X

Remarks by President Obama at Memorial Service for Former South African President Nelson Mandela, December 10, 2013. https://obamawhitehouse.archives.gov/the-press-office/2013/12/10/remarks-president-obama-memorial-service-former-south-african-president-

Rich, J. August 20, 2012. "The Upside of Uncertainty." *Huffington Post,* www.huffpost.com/entry/live-in-moment_b_1607664

Richards, C. September 25, 2017. "Want to Get Smarter Fast? Get In Over Your Head." *The New York Times,* www.nytimes.com/2017/09/25/your-money/want-to-get-smarter-fast-get-in-over-your-head.html

Rigby, D.K., S. Elk, and S. Berez. May 15, 2020. "Develop Agility that Outlasts the Pandemic." *Harvard Business Review,* https://hbr.org/2020/05/develop-agility-that-outlasts-the-pandemic

Roose, K. April 21, 2021. "Welcome to the YOLO Economy." *The New York Times,* www-nytimes-com.cdn.ampproject.org/c/s/www.nytimes.com/2021/04/21/technology/welcome-to-the-yolo-economy.amp.html?fbclid=IwAR1I1DHpcnTiY8liEYfOo3RgOqiyzcDXZEvCxCF6HSH1_9IRb-_eyEnnbkE

Rosenthal, B.M. May 19, 2019. "They Were Conned': How Reckless Loans Devastated a Generation of Taxi Drivers." *The New York Time,* www.nytimes.com/2019/05/19/nyregion/nyc-taxis-medallions-suicides.html

Roush, M. May 11, 2021. "Ava "Good is the Minimum. It's the Baseline. You Have To Be So Much More Than Good. And Even if you're Great and Lucky." *TV Insider,* www.tvinsider.com/998079/hacks-hbo-max-review-matt-roush/

Ruddock, S., and R. Craig. April 23, 2021. "Since Colleges are Failing to Prepare Students for Tech Jobs, it is Time to Bring Back Apprenticeships." *Tech Crunch,* https://techcrunch.com/2021/04/23/since-colleges-are-failing-to-prepare-students-for-tech-jobs-its-time-to-bring-back-apprenticeships/

Samuel, S. June 09, 2020. "Quarantine has Changed Us—and It's Not All Bad." *VOX,* www.vox.com/future-perfect/2020/6/9/21279258/coronavirus-pandemic-new-quarantine-habits

Sayed, A. April 27, 2021. "COVID has Revealed the Essential Value of the Digital 'Pivot'." *Fortune,* https://fortune.com/2021/04/27/covid-digital-transformation-pivot-bmc-software-automation-ai/

Schawbel, D. August 04, 2015. "Geoff Colvin: Why Humans Will Triumph Over Machines." *Forbes.*

Schiano, R. August 06, 2018. "Let Go of Yesterday." *Psychology Today,* www.psychologytoday.com/us/blog/in-the-face-adversity/201808/let-go-yesterday

Schrage, M. Winter 2003. "Daniel Kahneman: The Thought Leader Interview." *strategy + business,* www.strategy-business.com/article/03409?gko=d1233

Schuessler, J. October 11, 2017. "MacArthur Foundation Names 2017 'Genius' Grant Winners." *The New York Times,* www.nytimes.com/2017/10/11/arts/macarthur-genius-grants.html

Schwab, K. May 04, 2021. "Reevaluating Your Career? You're Not Alone." *Marketplace.* www.marketplace.org/2021/05/04/reevaluating-your-career-youre-not-alone/

Schwartz, L. n.d. "Didrikson was a Woman Ahead of Her Time." *ESPN,* www.espn.com/sportscentury/features/00014147.html

Schwartzberg, E. April 27, 2021. "Get Set for a Tsunami of People Changing Jobs Once the Pandemic Ebbs, Experts Say." *Seattle Times,* www.seattletimes.com/explore/careers/get-set-for-a-tsunami-of-people-changing-jobs-once-pandemic-ebbs-experts-say/

Schwarz, N. n.d. "Self-Care for People Who Don't Have Time for Self-Care." https://mindfulartstudio.com/self-care-in-no-time/

Seelye, K.Q. January 07, 2021. "Alex Trebek, Longtime Host of 'Jeopardy!,' Dies at 80." *The New York Times,* www.nytimes.com/2020/11/08/arts/television/alex-trebek-dead.html

Seneca, *Moral Letters to Lucilius.* "Letter XVIII: On Festivals and Fasting." 65 AD, https://sites.google.com/site/thestoiclife/the_teachers/seneca/letters/018

Seppälä, E., and K. Cameron. December 01, 2015. "Proof that Positive Work Cultures are More Productive." *Harvard Business Review,* https://hbr.org/2015/12/proof-that-positive-work-cultures-are-more-productive

Shallcross, A.J., A. Troy and I.B. Mauss. n.d. "Change Your Feelings or Leave Them Be? (or both?): How Best to Regulate Emotions in the Face of Stress." https://eerlab.berkeley.edu/pdf/papers/inpress_Shallcross_Emerging_Trends.pdf

Shaping the Trends of Our Times. 2020. "United Nations." www.un.org/development/desa/publications/wp-content/uploads/sites/10/2020/09/20-124-UNEN-75Report-1.pdf (accessed September 2020).

"Skills for 2030: Conceptual Learning Framework." The Organization for Economic and Community Development, 2019. www.oecd.org/education/2030-project/teaching-and-learning/learning/skills/Skills_for_2030_concept_note.pdf

Slouching Towards Bethlehem. https://en.wikipedia.org/wiki/Slouching_Towards_Bethlehem

Small, J. April 03, 2021. "Volatility, Uncertainty, Complexity and Ambiguity, How to Plan for the World of the Future." *FE News*, www.fenews.co.uk/fevoices/66344-volatility-uncertainty-complexity-and-ambiguity-how-to-plan-for-the-world-of-the-future

Smialek, J. May 14, 2020. "Poor Americans Hit Hardest by Job Losses Amid Lockdowns, Fed Says." *New York Times*, www.nytimes.com/2020/05/14/business/economy/coronavirus-jobless-unemployment.html

Smith, P. February 22, 2020. "Mark Ruffalo: 'Hollywood has been White Supremacist for 100 years'." *Independent.* www.independent.co.uk/arts-entertainment/films/features/mark-ruffalo-interview-dark-waters-avengers-marvel-trump-kevin-feige-boris-johnson-a9351101.html

"Soft Skills vs. Hard Skills in the Workplace." *Glassdoor*, n.d. www.glassdoor.com/blog/guide/soft-skills-vs-hard-skills/

St. Amour, M. December 17, 2020. "Few Positives in Final Fall Enrollment Numbers." *Inside Higher Ed*, www.insidehighered.com/news/2020/12/17/final-fall-enrollment-numbers-show-pandemics-full-impact

"Status quo bias." Behavioral Economics, www.behavioraleconomics.com/resources/mini-encyclopedia-of-be/status-quo-bias/

Stearns, P.N. 1998. "Why Study History." *1998 American Historical Association*, www.historians.org/about-aha-and-membership/aha-history-and-archives/historical-archives/why-study-history-(1998)

Stolzenberg, E.B., et al. 2020. "The American Freshman: National Norms Fall 2019, Cooperative Institutional Research Program at the Higher Education Research Institute at UCLA, www.heri.ucla.edu/monographs/TheAmericanFreshman2019.pdf

Synnott, M. October 03, 2018. "Exclusive: Alex Honnold Completes the Most Dangerous Free-Solo Ascent Ever." *National Geographic*, www.nationalgeographic.com/adventure/article/most-dangerous-free-solo-climb-yosemite-national-park-el-capitan

Talbert, R. November 04, 2010. "Want a Job? Major in What You Enjoy." *Chronicle of Higher Education*, www.chronicle.com/blognetwork/castingoutnines/want-a-job-major-in-what-you-enjoy?cid2=gen_login_refresh&cid=gen_sign_in

Tay, L. June 01, 2020. "Focusing Illusion." *Purdue University blog*, www.purdue.edu/stepstoleaps/explore/well-being-tips/2020_0601.php

Tetlock, P.E. 2006. Expert Political Judgment: How Good Is It? How Can We Know? www.amazon.com/Expert-Political-Judgment-Good-Know/dp/0691128715

The American Freshman: National Norms. n.d. www.heri.ucla.edu/monographs/TheAmericanFreshman2019.pdf

The Conference Board. April 2021. "A US Workforce Training Plan for the Postpandemic Economy." www.ced.org/solutions-briefs/a-us-workforce-training-plan-for-the-postpandemic-economy#section4

"The Enterprise Guide to Closing the Skills Gap." *IBM*, www.ibm.com/thought-leadership/institute-business-value/report/closing-skills-gap

"The Future of Work After COVID-19." *McKinsey*, February 18, 2021. www.mckinsey.com/featured-insights/future-of-work/the-future-of-work-after-covid-19

"The Future of Work: Workplace Trends for 2021 and Beyond." *National Law Review*. February 22, 2021. www.natlawreview.com/article/future-work-workplace-trends-2021-and-beyond

The OECD Future of Education and Skills 2030: Conceptual Learning Framework.

"The Making of Full Metal Jacket." *YouTube*, July 16, 2014. www.youtube.com/watch?v=XRkyKYz5SYM

"The Social Enterprise in a World Disrupted: Leading The Shift from Survive To Thrive." 2021 Deloitte Global Human Capital Trends, www2.deloitte.com/content/dam/insights/us/articles/6935_2021-HC-Trends/di_human-capital-trends.pdf

"The Story Behind the Iconic 'Kiss of Life' Photo." April 17, 2017. https://historydaily.org/story-behind-iconic-kiss-life-photo

"The Work of the Future: Building Better Jobs in an Age of Intelligent Machines." 2020. *MIT*, https://workofthefuture.mit.edu/wp-content/uploads/2021/01/2020-Final-Report4.pdf

Tiefenbacher, W. December 31, 2019. "Strategic Management: How and Why to Redefine Organizational Strategy in Today's VUCA World." *CQ Net*, www.ckju.net/en/blog/strategic-management-how-and-why-redefine-organizational-strategy-todays-vuca-world/58699

Todd, S. May 21, 2021. "An Economist's Rule for Making Tough Life Decisions." *Quartz*, https://getpocket.com/explore/item/an-economist-s-rule-for-making-tough-life-decisions?utm_source=pocket-newtab

Tolle, E. 2004. "The Power of Now: A Guide to Spiritual Enlightenment." www.amazon.com/Power-Now-Guide-Spiritual-Enlightenment/dp/1577314808/ref=sr_1_1?dchild=1&keywords=the+power+of+now&qid=1621267452&sr=8-1

Tolle, E. 2005. "A New Earth: Awakening to Your Life's Purpose." www.amazon.com/New-Earth-Awakening-Lifes-Purpose/dp/0525948023/ref=tmm_hrd_swatch_0?_encoding=UTF8&qid=&sr=

Trott, D. April 09, 2008. "Paul Arden." https://davetrott.co.uk/2008/04/paul-arden/

Tsioulcas, A. December 19, 2015. "Remembering Kurt Masur, The Conductor Who Rebuilt The New York Philharmonic." *NPR*, www.npr.org/sections/

deceptivecadence/2015/12/19/460392051/remembering-kurt-masur-the-conductor-who-rebuilt-the-new-york-philharmonic

Tutu, D. 2000. "No Future Without Forgiveness." www.amazon.com/Future-Without-Forgiveness-Desmond-Tutu/dp/0385496907

Twenge, J.M. 2014. "Generation Me - Revised and Updated: Why Today"s Young Americans Are More Confident, Assertive, Entitled--and More Miserable Than Ever Before." www.amazon.com/Generation-Americans-Confident-Assertive-Entitled/dp/1476755566

Unemployment Rates, OECD—Updated: April 2021.www.oecd.org/newsroom/unemployment-rates-oecd-update-april-2021.htm (accessed April 12, 2021).

Upston, C. September 28, 2020. "Reimagining Blended Learning in the New World of Work." *Training zone*, www.trainingzone.co.uk/deliver/training/reimagining-blended-learning-in-the-new-world-of-work

Vajda, P. March 04, 2016. "Why you Need Equanimity." *Management Issues*, www.management-issues.com/opinion/5992/why-you-need-equanimity/

Vidal, T. January 27, 2016. "The Man Who Can Drive Himself Further Once the Effort Gets Painful is the Man Who Will Win." *LinkedIn*, www.linkedin.com/pulse/man-who-can-drive-himself-further-once-effort-gets-painful-vidal/

Walmsley, T., A. Rose, and D. Wei. December 10, 2020. "The Impacts of the Coronavirus on the Economy of the United States." *Economics of Disasters and Climate Change*, https://link.springer.com/article/10.1007/s41885-020-00080-1

Warrell, M. July 15, 2015. "Why Embracing Uncertainty Is Critical to Your Success." www.forbes.com/sites/margiewarrell/2015/07/21/why-embracing-uncertainty-is-critical-to-your-success/?sh=4b2a75da673c

Wayland, M. April 20, 2021. "GM's New Remote Work Plan for Employees is Ambiguous, yet Surprisingly Simple: 'Work Appropriately'." *CNBC*, www.cnbc.com/2021/04/20/gms-simple-message-to-employees-about-return-to-work-work-appropriately.html

Weldon, M. August 30, 2020. "COVID-19 Has Made Me Rethink Much of My Life." *NBC*, www.nbcnews.com/think/opinion/covid-19-has-made-me-rethink-much-my-life-including-ncna1238289

"What Unseen Megatrends Will Shape Your Transformation?" EY, www.ey.com/en_gl

White, A. November 01, 2017. "Thinking is the Hardest Work there is, Which is Probably the Reason, So Few Engage in it." *Henry Ford, LinkedIn*. www.linkedin.com/pulse/thinking-hardest-work-which-probably-reason-so-few-engage-white/

Wikipedia Entry. 2019. "2019 College Admissions Bribery Scandal." https://en.wikipedia.org/wiki/2019_college_admissions_bribery_scandal (accessed March 12, 2021).

Wiles, J. May 22, 2020. "Build the Workforce You Need Post-COVID-19." *Gartner*, www.gartner.com/smarterwithgartner/build-the-workforce-you-need-post-covid-19/

Wiles, J. October 23, 2020. "Gartner Top 3 Priorities for HR Leaders in 2021." *Gartner*, www.gartner.com/smarterwithgartner/gartner-top-3-priorities-for-hr-leaders-in-2021/

Wilkie, D. October 21, 2019. "Employers Say College Grads Lack Hard Skills, Too." *SHRM*, www.shrm.org/ResourcesAndTools/hr-topics/employee-relations/Pages/Employers-Say-College-Grads-Lack-Hard-Skills-Too.aspx

"Workforce of the Future: The Competing Forces Shaping 2030." *PWC*, 2019, www.pwc.com/gx/en/services/people-organisation/publications/workforce-of-the-future.html

World Economic Forum. 2021. "The Global Risks Report, 2021 edition." www3.weforum.org/docs/WEF_The_Global_Risks_Report_2021.pdf

World Economic Forum. October 2020. "The Future of Jobs Report, 2020." www.weforum.org/docs/WEF_Future_of_Jobs_2020.pdf

World Health Organization Website. n.d. "Listings of WHO's Response to COVID-19." www.who.int/news/item/29-06-2020-covidtimeline (accessed February 28, 2021).

World Health Organization Website. n.d. "Naming the Coronavirus Disease (COVID-19) and the Virus that Causes it." www.who.int/emergencies/diseases/novel-coronavirus-2019/technical-guidance/naming-the-coronavirus-disease-(covid-2019)-and-the-virus-that-causes-it (accessed February 28, 2021).

Worley, C.G., and C. Jules. June 16, 2020. "COVID-19's Uncomfortable Revelations About Agile and Sustainable Organizations in a VUCA World." *The Journal of Applied Behavioral Science,* https://journals.sagepub.com/doi/full/10.1177/0021886320936263

www.goodreads.com/book/show/3521748-letters-1

www.goodreads.com/quotes/14033-question-i-am-interested-in-so-many-things-and-i

www.oecd.org/education/2030-project/teaching-and-learning/learning/skills/Skills_for_2030_concept_note.pdf The Organization for Economic Cooperation and Development is an Intergovernmental Economic Organization with 37 Member Countries, Founded in 1961 to Stimulate Economic Progress and World Trade.

Wyer, K. January 23, 2013. "Survey: More Freshmen than Ever Say They go to College to Get Better Jobs, Make More Money." UCLS press release, https://newsroom.ucla.edu/releases/heri-freshman-survey-242619 In their response to this data Michael B. Horn and Bob Moesta suggest going to college to get a job is "woefully incomplete" and should consider other factors such as the student doing what is expected of them, for the student to get away, and to extend themselves. Upon a close read of their work, however, Horn and Moesta link each of their factors back to a student's ability to get a job. So, in the end, students do indeed go to college to get a job or position themselves to get a better job as opposed to having just a high school diploma. The nuances Horn and Moesta found are important, but they lack any ability to significantly alter the UCLA longitudinal study.

Yates, S. January 14, 2021. "Meet Ashley Lamothe, the HBCU Grad Who Became Chick-Fil-A's Youngest Black Franchise Owner At Age 26." *Afro Tech*, https://afrotech.com/meet-ashley-lamothe-the-hbcu-grad-who-became-chick-fil-as-youngest-black-franchise-owner-at-age-26

"Zoom Sees More Growth After 'Unprecedented' 2020." *BBC*, March 01, 2021. www.bbc.com/news/business-56247489

About the Author

Michael Edmondson, PhD, is the Dean, College of Professional Studies, Dean, Division of Professional Education and Lifelong Learning, and Director, NJCU at Fort Monmouth at New Jersey City University. Author of *Agility: Management Principles for A Volatile World* (Business Experts Press, 2020), *The Relevance of Humanities to the 21st Century Workplace* (Business Experts Press, 2019), *Strategic Thinking and Writing* (Business Experts Press, 2018), *Success: Theory and Practice* (Business Experts press, 2016), *Major in Happiness: Debunking the College Major Fallacies* (Business Experts Press, 2015), and *Marketing Your Value: 9 Steps to Navigate Your Career* (Business Experts Press, 2015), he has over 30 years of experience in both the nonprofit and for-profit sectors. He has a PhD in History from Temple University, an MA in History from Villanova University, and a BA in History from Cabrini University.

Related books: Scott Galloway's *Post Corona: From Crisis to Opportunity*, published in November 2020 is the only book available focusing on the ongoing global pandemic and serves as an assessment of the global marketplace rather than an employee training program. Examples of titles that focus specifically on employee training include *The Art and Science of Training* (2017) by Elaine Biech, *Kirkpatrick's Four Levels of Training Evaluation* (2016) by James D. Kirkpatrick, *Improving Performance Through Learning: A Practical Guide for Designing High Performance Learning Journeys* (2019) by Robert O. Brinkerhoff, Anne M. Apking, and Edward W. Boon, and *ATD's Action Guide to Talent Development: A Practical Approach to Building Your Organization's TD Effort* (2018) by Elaine Biech.

Index

OTHER TITLES IN THE HUMAN RESOURCE MANAGEMENT AND ORGANIZATIONAL BEHAVIOR COLLECTION

Michael Provitera, Editor

- *Breaking the Proactive Paradox* by Baker Tim
- *The Modern Trusted Advisor* by MacKay Nancy and Weiss Alan
- *Achieving Success as a 21st Century Manager* by Dean E. Frost
- *How to Create Awesome Workplaces* by Samuel Gladstone Leslie
- *A.I. and Remote Working* by Miller Tony
- *Best Boss!* by Ferguson Duncan, Toni M. Pristo, and John Furcon
- *Managing for Accountability* by Curry Lynne
- *Fundamentals of Level Three Leadership* by Clawson James G.S.
- *Emotional Connection: The EmC Strategy* by Gershfeld Lola and Sedehi Ramin
- *Civility at Work* by Bayer Lewena
- *Lean on Civility* by Masotti Christian and Bayer Lewena
- *Agility* by Edmondson Michael
- *Strengths Oriented Leadership* by Beadle Matt
- *Leadership in Disruptive Times* by Bawany Sattar

Concise and Applied Business Books

The Collection listed above is one of 30 business subject collections that Business Expert Press has grown to make BEP a premiere publisher of print and digital books. Our concise and applied books are for...

- Professionals and Practitioners
- Faculty who adopt our books for courses
- Librarians who know that BEP's Digital Libraries are a unique way to offer students ebooks to download, not restricted with any digital rights management
- Executive Training Course Leaders
- Business Seminar Organizers

Business Expert Press books are for anyone who needs to dig deeper on business ideas, goals, and solutions to everyday problems. Whether one print book, one ebook, or buying a digital library of 110 ebooks, we remain the affordable and smart way to be business smart. For more information, please visit www.businessexpertpress.com, or contact sales@businessexpertpress.com.